EARTH MYSTERIES

earth mysteries

MICHAEL HOWARD

ROBERT HALE · LONDON

© *Michael Howard 1990*
First published in Great Britain 1990

Robert Hale Limited
Clerkenwell House
Clerkenwell Green
London EC1R 0HT

British Library Cataloguing in Publication Data

Howard, Michael, *1948–*
Earth mysteries.
1. Great Britain. Prehistoric antiquities
I. Title
936.1'01

ISBN 0–7090–3933–6

Photoset in North Wales by
Derek Doyle & Associates, Mold, Clwyd.
Printed in Great Britain by
St Edmundsbury Press Ltd, Bury St Edmunds, Suffolk.
Bound by WBC Bookbinders Limited.

CONTENTS

for
LINDA
who opened my eyes
and taught me so much

ILLUSTRATIONS

LINE DRAWINGS

ACKNOWLEDGEMENTS

Paul Devereux/Ian Thomson: 1, 21, 23. Gerald Ponting/Janet and
Colin Bord: 2. Janet and Colin Bord: 3, 8, 11, 13-15, 17, 20. Cadw:
Welsh Historic Monuments (Crown Copyright): 4. English Heritage:
5-7. Egyptian State Tourist Board: 9. The National Trust
Photographic Library: 10. Roger Vlitos/Janet and Colin Bord: 12.
Anthony Weir/Janet and Colin Bord: 16. Wolfgang Heigl: 18. French
Government Tourist Board: 19. The Ley Hunter: 22. Mrs M.
Lethbridge: 24-6.

INTRODUCTION

My purpose in writing this book is to introduce the reader to the fascinating subject of Earth Mysteries. This is a term which arose in the 1970s to describe the general study of ley lines or the alignment of ancient sites, stone circles and standing stones, the hill figures of southern England, the secret powers and occult symbolism of pyramids, and the existence of terrestrial zodiacs.

Although the term 'Earth Mysteries' is only of recent origin, the study of the subjects gathered together under this heading has a long history. As early as the eighteenth century, researchers such as the Rev. William Stukeley were engaged in the study of prehistoric sites, including the great circle of Stonehenge on Salisbury Plain in Wiltshire. He concluded that this megalithic monument was aligned to the rising sun and had been used by ancient people as a primitive calendar. Stukeley was a pioneer who blazed the trail for many other Earth Mysteries researchers who were to follow up his theories on the astronomical alignment of prehistoric circles and standing stones.

When the megalithic or 'great stones' culture erected the stone circles across the British Isles and Europe thousands of years ago, Earth Mysteries researchers believe they selected special sites which were already regarded as holy or sacred and were used for religious purposes. These sites were considered special because they were power centres where the natural energy of the Earth was concentrated. This energy was harnessed and used by the priests of the megalithic culture for purposes which can only be described in our modern terms of reference as 'magical'.

Until a few years ago this concept of the magical use of Earth energies, which achieved considerable popularity during the counter-culture years of the 1960s and was largely dismissed then by orthodox archaeologists as romantic fantasy, was not considered a suitable subject for in-depth study. However, the times have changed and today scientific research carried out at stone circles by members of the Dragon Project, funded and organized by *The Ley Hunter* magazine, has provided proof of the existence of Earth energy as a tangible force which can be measured using modern technological methods.

The purpose behind Earth Mysteries research is to collate the available information on the various ancient sites so that an overall pattern can be perceived. This information ranges from the purely technical details of measuring sites and calculating alignments to investigating the folklore, legends, religious traditions and local history of a sacred place. It is obvious that the ancients who erected the stone circles, carved the hill figures, excavated the holy wells and laid out the terrestrial zodiacs did so for a reason which was based on a spiritual vision of their relationship with the landscape in which they lived and their perceived role in the cosmos as human beings.

Although it is possible to study Earth Mysteries from a purely academic and practical level, this materialistic approach cannot provide the complete answer to the ancient riddles concealed in the landscape. In fact, it is the spiritual aspects of Earth Mysteries research which attract most people to the subject.

This book offers a history of Earth Mysteries research, describes the major ancient sites associated with it and provides advice on the practical aspects of exploring our sacred landscape. By using the information in these pages, I hope the reader will emerge at the end of our magical mystery tour fully equipped to undertake the quest for the clues to the mystical past which, although concealed, are still a living power in the land.

Michael Howard
West Wales, 1989

1

LEY LINES
AND
DRAGON POWER

In 1921 a 66-year-old Herefordshire man called Alfred
Watkins made a discovery which was to revolutionize
archaeology and the way modern man viewed the landscape.
This discovery was based on the fact that many prehistoric
sites in the British countryside are aligned in straight lines.
Watkins was not the first researcher to stumble upon this
simple fact, but his detailed recording of the information, his
dedication and his theories of the origin of these alignments
place him in a different league from earlier pioneers in this
field of unorthodox archaeology. His personal vision of the ley
lines, as the alignments became to be known, provides the first
comprehensive picture of a spiritual system practised by the
ancients to control the natural energy forces in the landscape
and make contact with cosmic influences.

Before he discovered the ley lines, Watkins was already
regarded as an interesting character and was a respected local
figure. He was a magistrate, inventor and pioneer photo-
grapher who possessed a wide knowledge of local history and

folklore. Although he was later to be dismissed as an eccentric by academics, who rejected his work on leys as the product of a crankish old man, what we know about his life and career suggests that Watkins was a respected and talented member of the community who combined a successful career with a wide range of spare-time interests and hobbies.

As a business partner in his family firm of flour millers and brewers, Watkins was provided with many opportunities to travel widely in the Herefordshire countryside visiting clients. As an amateur antiquarian, he was interested in the ancient history of the county and had an intimate knowledge of the prehistoric monuments in the area. In the summer of 1921, while touring the county on a business trip, Watkins suddenly realized, in a moment which he was later to describe as 'a flash of insight', that many of the ancient sites were aligned in straight lines.

It is tempting to interpret this sudden insight as a mystical vision, except that, for all his knowledge of the religious beliefs of our ancient ancestors, Watkins was basically a down-to-earth person who approached his study of the leys in a rational and scientific manner. For instance, on his return from one particular business trip he noted on an Ordnance Survey map that several sites were arranged in a straight line. He did not take this fact for granted but later confirmed it by physically taking sitings from a hilltop.

This method of first plotting an alignment on a map and then actually confirming its existence on the ground led Watkins to the discovery that his insight was correct, that ancient sites had been apparently placed in the landscape in straight lines so that they aligned. Watkins noted that these sites included megalithic circles, standing stones, prehistoric burial mounds, holy wells, beacon hills, pre-Reformation churches – which were often sited on the foundations of pagan temples or sacred groves – and medieval manor houses and castles – which had been built on Iron Age hill-forts or prehistoric earthworks.

When Watkins began to gather material on these

alignments, he at first called them 'old straight tracks'. This was because he initially thought his researches had revealed a lost system of prehistoric trackways which connected ancient settlements and religious sites. In recognition of this fact, he called his first book on the subject, published in 1925, *The Old Straight Track*. According to Watkins, these trackways had markers added to them at a later date. The markers were previously the sites of the pagan worship of the Nature gods and goddesses associated with the seasonal cycle of the natural year. Over the centuries these pre-Christian shrines were replaced by early churches, castles and medieval manor houses.

Originally Watkins' theory of the old straight tracks involved a prehistoric system of nationwide communication using beacon hills and the alignments. In the neolithic or New Stone Age Watkins believed humankind was instinctively attracted to hilltops which offered a clear vantage-point from which the topographical features of the surrounding land could be viewed and surveyed. In the prehistoric period, when the land was heavily forested, the high points of hills provided the only areas from which a clear view of the countryside could be obtained for defensive purposes. Hilltops also acquired a religious importance because of ancient beliefs crediting them with being the dwelling-place of the gods of storm and wind who had descended from the sky in primeval times.

This first explanation for the alignments postulated by Watkins involved a person in prehistoric times surveying the surrounding land from the summit of a hill. This surveyor would have been aware of any natural markers in the countryside below which might be aligned to a hill across the valley. The surveyor travelled to the second hill and erected a small mound of stones to create an artificial marker. He or she then went down into the valley and built a larger stone monument to act as a half-way marker between the two sighting-points.

With the passage of time, more sophisticated methods were adopted to align different sites. These included the development of primitive technological aids such as measuring-rods or sighting-staves and eventually crude compasses. Gradually, as this surveying work took on a more structured nature, it became linked with spiritual concepts of the sacredness of the land and the worship of the deities of Nature and fertility. A system of trackways was developed across the countryside linking important natural and artificial sites which had a sacred significance to the ancients. This religious aspect of Earth Mysteries research became an increasingly important feature of Watkins' ideas about alignments as his theories developed over the years.

Watkins' original idea of ley lines as ancient trackways had been preceded by the work of H. Hippisley Cox, who had published his findings about what he described as 'green roads' in 1914. Cox formulated the idea that the Iron Age hill-forts scattered across southern England were markers linking a complex pattern of trackways which criss-crossed the countryside. He speculated that these hill-forts which had been used by the Celts were previously sites of Stone Age settlements and that the common meeting-places of these trackways were prehistoric burial mounds, Bronze Age stone circles and medieval dew ponds.

The 'green roads' located by Cox included several trackways which have been in use since ancient times. These have survived and today form the basis for the network of major national footpaths used by ramblers. They include the South Downs Way which passes from Hampshire across the Sussex downs. This trackway intersects several important prehistoric and Iron Age sites, including the mysterious Chanctonbury Ring which may possibly have originated as a druidic sacred grove. Chanctonbury has traditionally been associated with ghostly happenings, the manifestation of the Devil and witchcraft rites. The trackway also passes through the evocatively named Devil's Dyke and Ditchling Beacon, where the spectral hounds of the Celtic underworld have been sighted, before ending at Beachy Head, where the cliffs are a popular place for suicides.

Another famous trackway which was an ancient green road is The Ridgeway. This links several famous sites, including the stone circles of Avebury in Wiltshire, the burial mound of Wayland's Smithy and the White Horse of Uffington in Berkshire. In the same general area, another green road connects Stonehenge, possibly the most famous stone circle in the British Isles, with nearby Old Sarum. The latter was originally an Iron Age earthwork which in medieval times was the site of the first Salisbury Cathedral before it was moved to its present site in the thirteenth century.

Eventually Watkins discarded the term 'old straight track' to describe the alignments and adopted instead an old Saxon word, *ley*. This word is spelt in several ways, including lay, lea, lee and leigh. According to the *Oxford English Dictionary* (1976 edition), it means 'land temporarily under grass'. It particularly refers to an enclosed field or pasture, although the Old English derivation of *laege* signifies 'a tract of open ground, especially grassland'.

Watkins was never entirely happy with this word to describe the alignments and spends several pages in his first book analysing its meaning. In the end he decided to use it because many of the alignments and straight tracks did pass through woodland clearings on their route from site to site. Watkins had also noted that the word *laye* was an old-fashioned term for 'fire' or 'a flame'. In the East, *laya yoga* was a magical technique for the raising of the *kundalini*, the serpent force within the *chakra*, the psychic centre at the base of the human spine. This energy allegedly rose up the spine into the brain, causing the spiritual enlightenment of the yogi. It has been suggested that the evocation of Earth energies, sometimes called the dragon power, along the power centres (*chakras*) of the landscape, forms part of an ancient esoteric tradition connected with this form of yoga. However, it was Watkins' belief that the ancients used fires lit on hilltops as both a signalling device and a method of surveying straight lines. In ancient mythology fire also had a spiritual significance, representing divine wisdom received from heaven or the gods by religious teachers.

It was also Watkins' idea that the straight lines in the landscape were astronomically aligned to the rising and setting of the sun, the moon and specific stars and constellations. This concept of alignments as astronomical pointers was not entirely an original one. In formulating this theory Watkins appears to have been influenced by the pioneering work of Sir Norman Lockyer at the end of the nineteenth century. Lockyer's research will be examined in Chapter 2, dealing with astro-archaeology.

The sudden realization by Watkins of the existence and significance of leys has been interpreted by some more imaginative researchers in terms of a mystical revelation. Although very little is known about Watkins' religious beliefs, he does seem to have been very much aware of the spiritual dimension of his discoveries, even though he approached the subject from a scientific viewpoint. His understanding of the sacredness of the land is summed up in the following quotation which is credited to Rudyard Kipling and was included in *The Old Straight Track*: 'She [Britain] is not only common earth, water, wood or air but Merlin's isle of grammarye [magic].'

Because Watkins had an intuitive awareness that leys had a non-material foundation, he represented their ancient surveyors as members of a special elite who possessed considerable esoteric knowledge. He regarded the ley men – as he called them, although there is no reason to suppose their ranks did not include women – as a type of priesthood or secret society with magical or occult (hidden) powers. Watkins believed these ley men had 'class names' which designated their calling. He identified three of these names as Dod, Cole and Black and cites instances where they appear in place-names associated with leys and ancient sites.

The word 'Cole' was derived by Watkins from an obscure Old English word for a juggler or magician. It can also mean a diviner or a person who can foretell the future, a prophet, a wizard (wise man) or a sorcerer. Watkins believed 'cole' was an ancient word which once had important sacred, magical and religious significance but had become corrupted and debased through centuries of misuse. He claimed to have traced the word back to the Aryan or Indo-European root language which developed into Celtic, and identified it in Welsh as *coel*, meaning 'an omen'. In ancient Wales the *coelbren* was a magical alphabet used by the Druids in a form which was similar to the Anglo-Saxon or Germanic runes. The *coelbren* was used as a secret code to pass on esoteric knowledge between druidic initiates and as a method to divination or predicting the future. *Coelcerth* in Old Welsh was a term used to describe a beacon fire lit to warn of danger. This links with Watkins' theory that at some stage in their development leys were an effective cross-country communication system.

The second name highlighted by Watkins as being associated with the prehistoric surveyors was Dod. This strange word has links with the Old English *tot* or *toot*, which means 'a rounded hill'. There may be a link here with the female breast – hence the slang word 'tit' – and the pagan belief in the Great Mother or Earth goddess. In Irish folklore there are references to prominent rounded hills which are known as the Paps (or nipples) of Danu. This is a reference to the Irish mother goddess Danu and the pagan concept of the land as the body of the goddess. In Old English *tot* means a lookout place, and *totoem* is the site of a hill-fort.

Watkins also traced the word Dod back to the Welsh (Celtic) *dodi*, meaning 'to lay' and identified it as an obsolete word for a staff or club. He speculated that the ley men used staves or rods for sighting-purposes when they were surveying. These sighting-rods, he further believed, became corrupted in popular folk-belief until they became the stock-in-trade of the magicians, wizards and 'cole men' from Celtic times to the Middle Ages.

The staff, rod or wand of the prehistoric shaman (priest) was an important ritual tool representing divine authority and the power of the magician to control his environment. When the tribal king or queen adopted many of the attributes of the priesthood, they also adopted the ritual wand, which became their sceptre of royal office. Following the replacement of paganism by Christianity, the wand became the symbol of those who still practised the Old Religion. One of its manifestations was the traditional besom or broomstick owned by the village wisewomen, or witches, who peddled herbal remedies and who, as midwives and layers-out of the dead, ruled over the forces of life and death.

In folklore witches were credited with flying through the air on their broomsticks. This could be seen as a connection between the witches – whose name is derived from a Saxon word meaning 'wise ones' – and the Earth energy which flows along the ley lines. In both folk-tradition and actuality, the witches were associated with ancient sites and used stone circles and burial mounds – known to them as 'faery hills' – as meeting-places. It is recorded that Welsh witches held their revels at the Penmaenmawr megalithic circle until a voice spoke from one of the stones, causing two of the coven to fall down dead and another to go mad. This folk-tale suggests a warning about the misuse of Earth energy.

Witches also traditionally gathered at the Rollright Stones on the Warwickshire–Oxfordshire border, Cadbury hill-fort in Somerset (which is reputed to have been King Arthur's Camelot), the Five Knolls burial mound in Bedfordshire, the Auldean standing stones and the Ring of Brogar circle in Scotland, at Wayland's Smithy in Berkshire, the Merry Maidens stone circle and the Men-ar-Tol monument in Cornwall, Kit's Coty and the Coldrum Stones in Kent, Long Meg and her daughters' circle in Cumbria and the Long Rigg circle in Derbyshire.

The third name Watkins found significant in relation to leys was Black. He did not accept that the original meaning of this word was 'colourless due to an absence of light' (*OED*). Instead he claimed that it came from an Anglo-Saxon word, *blaec*, meaning 'shining white' or 'pale'. Watkins presumed that the description 'the black man' was an ancient title used to describe the special person who lit the beacon fires on the sacred hills. These fires celebrated the seasonal festivals of the pagan year.

If this is true, it is interesting that the high priest or master of the medieval witch covens, who personified the Horned God, was often called 'the man in black'. In Christian belief the man who led the coven in its orgiastic frolics was the Devil. One of his names was Lucifer, which, translated from Latin means 'the lightbringer'. When the Horned God presided over the witches' sabbat, it was said he wore a blazing torch between his horns.

Since the earliest times fire has been regarded as a sacred element and was worshipped by ancient cultures. Possibly the most sophisticated form of this worship was the Persian religion of Zoroastrianism, which was founded over 3,000 years ago. The sacred nature of fire was based upon its symbolism as a substitute for the sun, which was the object of worship by those patriarchal cultures which superseded the matrifocal, Goddess-worshipping societies of prehistoric Europe.

There are several natural and artificial landscape features identified by Watkins as markers indicating the presence of a ley and the subsequent progression of an alignment of sites across the countryside. These features were standing stones, megalithic circles, mounds, holy wells and sacred springs, beacon hills, earthworks, burial chambers, old crossroads, pre-Reformation churches, castles, medieval manor houses and groves of ancient trees. All these geographical reference points can be used by researchers to plot a ley accurately. The Earth Mysteries researcher will first trace the possible route of an alignment on an Ordnance Survey map – either 1:25000 or 1:50000 – and then confirm it by an actual field trip to survey it in the locality.

The basic equipment you initially need to mark out a ley on a map consists of a sharp pencil and a ruler. Opinions differ, but most people agree that 15–20 miles is a reasonable length to prove the existence of a ley. On an alignment of that length, the ideal number of identifiable and verifiable markers should be at least five. Obviously, the shorter the ley and the more markers the better.

When confirming the ley physically on a field trip, the equipment required includes weatherproof clothing, sturdy footwear, an OS map (preferably a small-scale one of the immediate area covered by the projected ley), a good compass and a pair of binoculars. A camera is an optional extra, as many researchers like to have a visual record of the ley-markers for future reference.

Naturally, when you are busy tracing the route of a possible alignment across the open countryside in overcrowded Britain, this may involve walking across farmland or other privately owned land. Unfortunately public footpaths do not always follow the routes of leys! Whenever possible, the researcher should ask permission from the landowner before venturing forth and should observe the Countryside Code at all times.

Technically it is essential that the ley be plotted on the OS map with some accuracy. It should be remembered that the ancient who surveyed the ley system did so with a high degree of precision. Therefore the markers along the route of the alignment should be in a straight line and not on either side of the proposed ley. This degree of accuracy can be difficult to gauge on a map and can be more accurately measured during a field trip. The phenomenon of edge alignment is recognized, whereby a ley passes the edge of a marker but always touches the parameter of the site.

Once the existence of a ley has been established, both on the map and in the field, historical research can be carried out. This includes an investigation of the local history and folklore of marker sites on the alignment. Local libraries and ancient history or archaeological societies should be able to provide suitable information in this direction. Where churches are found on a ley, parish records, guide-books and even a discreet chat with the vicar or priest can be helpful.

The principal markers to find on the route of a suspected alignment or ley are described below.

Standing Stones and Megalithic Circles

Watkins tended to describe standing stones as 'mark stones'. Stones of this type are usually small monoliths which are located at crossroads or alongside road verges. In the Middle Ages (500–1500 CE) these mark stones were used to indicate the distances on roads or parish boundaries, and they were often replaced by wayside crosses. In many cases the stones were uprooted by local farmers and used as gateposts for fields and farmyards.

Many of these mark stones have legends associated with them which can be useful keys to understanding their original pagan significance and use in the ley system. Folk-belief says they were put in place by giants, faeries or even the Devil. Watkins interpreted these tales as folk-memories of the creation of the ley system by the ancient surveyors. Where elemental spirits are not specifically referred to, folklorists have identified faeries with the aboriginal inhabitants of the British Isles. These small, dark, hairy people were greatly feared by the Celtic invaders as powerful magicians. With the arrival of the Celts they became associated with the dwarfs, goblins and faeries of folk-tradition and magical lore. Any reference to the Devil in the post-Christian period can be confidently regarded as a backhanded reference to the gods of the Old Religion.

The standing stones were especially identified with the creative force of the masculine aspect of the Earth energy which the ancients believed flowed along the ley lines. The shape of the stones made them an obvious phallic symbol, and their siting along the leys was regarded as a symbolic penetration of Mother Earth. In the pagan Old Religion the erect phallus was a representation of the fertilizing power of the sun and the life force which, according to ancient religious beliefs, permeates and sustains the universe.

Because of the stones' overtly phallic symbolism, sterile women who desired children would rub their naked bodies against the standing stones in an act of sympathetic magic, hoping to become pregnant. The monolith known as the King

Stone, which stands in a field opposite the Rollrights in Warwickshire, was often the scene of this type of folk-magic. Local women visited the site at the full moon and rubbed their breasts on the surface of the stone in the hope of conceiving children.

At crossroads in ancient Greece, standing stones were erected carved with phalli and serpents, in honour of the god Hermes or Mercury who was regarded as the personification of the male aspect of the Earth energy. Similar standing stones can be seen in Brittany carved with figures depicting the Celtic equivalent of Hermes. In Japan it was the ithyphallic god Chimata-no-kami who was the guardian of the roads and footpaths. His phallic images were set up at crossroads and venerated by female travellers in the time-honoured way as a representation of the life force.

In both megalithic and later historical times, standing stones were used as territory markers defining the boundaries of a tribe or community's land. These stones also had a spiritual meaning, as symbols of communication between earthly man and cosmic forces. Hermes was not only a phallic god but in ancient mythology took the role of the messenger of the gods who guided the dead to the underworld. Symbolically, the standing stone was a symbol of the cosmic tree or world pillar which provided the bridge between Middle Earth, the domain of humankind, and the realm of the gods.

Standing stones can be found in isolated, open countryside or in the vicinity of stone circles dating from the neolithic (New Stone Age) or Bronze Age periods. These circles can be found quite easily on an OS map, as most are clearly identifiable and are under the protection of English Heritage, the Department of the Environment or the National Trust. A few circles, such as the Rollrights and Long Meg, are still in private hands but they are open to the public and protected by the Ancient Monuments Act. Standing stones which are not near stone circles may be more difficult to locate, as many are not marked on maps and some have vanished in recent years with the increase in intensive farming methods.

Prehistoric Burial Mounds

Again these sites should be clearly visible on an OS map marked as tumulus (or tumuli, plural), barrows, cairns, cromlechs, dolmens or simply burial chambers. As these descriptions can cause some confusion, the following explanation of these terms might be useful.

A tumulus is usually a round burial mound dating from the Middle Bronze Age (*c*.1500–1200 BCE). Barrows are long mounds dating from the neolithic period (*c*.8,000–5,000 BCE) which usually contain a burial chamber made of stones. A cairn is a pyramid-shaped mound of stones erected to cover a burial place and dates from the Stone Age or even earlier. Cromlechs – from the Welsh, meaning 'flat' and 'crooked' – are the remnants of a burial chamber without its earth mound. They consist of a flat stone supported by several monolithic uprights. In Cornwall they are called dolmens, from the old Cornish meaning 'hole of stone'.

While burial mounds have been regarded by archaeologists as exclusively the sites of funeral rites and cremations, it has been suggested that they had a religious purpose which transcended this original use. The priesthood of the Old Religion practised a cult of the dead involving communication between the spirits of the departed, who dwelt in the Otherworld, and the living. These shamanistic initiation rites into the cult of the dead involved the neophyte's travelling in a trance state to the underworld. In a symbolic ritual of death and rebirth, he or she then communicated with the gods and the spirits of the tribal ancestors.

These religious practices have led to speculation that some burial chambers were used for initiation rites. One example may have been the Pentre Ifan cromlech in Dyfed, West Wales. This imposing structure stands in an isolated position overlooking the sea, the Preseli hills and the valley of Nevern. According to local folk-tradition, in Celtic times the area was the site of a druidic college, and Pentre Ifan, known locally as 'the womb of the goddess Ceridwen', was used for initiations.

In addition to burial mounds, Watkins highlighted any

other type of mound or hillock which can be found in the landscape as a possible ley marker. These included the various earthworks or henges surrounding sacred places or ancient human settlements. Watkins believed that many of these mounds were originally inside deep ditches or moats filled with water. These rings of water would have shone brightly, reflecting sunlight or moonshine, and created a valuable sighting-point for travellers.

Mounds and earthworks were often used in ancient times as places for moots, which were the tribal assemblies where laws were made and matters of public concern discussed. This practice dates from pre-Christian times and is still perpetuated on the Isle of Man, where the Manx parliament convenes every year on a sacred mound. In rural England the mounds were the focal point of the local community and used as the traditional site for country fairs and rustic markets. These events were celebrated on the quarter and cross-quarter days of the agricultural calendar, which coincidentally correspond with the dates of pagan festivals practised by the Celts and the megalithic people.

Wells and Springs

During Watkins' extensive research into the ley-line system which criss-crosses the British countryside, he often found that holy wells and sacred springs marked the beginning and the end of leys. They also acted as what he called 'secondary markers' on alignments.

Thousands of years before wells were accepted into Christian mythology as sites of healing, miracles and saint veneration, they were regarded by the pagan Old Religion as natural shrines. Many wells and springs were dedicated to the worship of the Celtic goddesses and were attributed with healing, fertility and psychic powers. Holy wells can therefore be regarded as ideal markers for prehistoric alignments, as they were recognized by the ancients as power centres and used by them for religious purposes.

Beacon Hills

When he was forming his first theories about leys, Watkins noted that prominent hills used for lighting beacon fires were important markers on alignments. The ancients not only used beacons as a signalling method but also had a religious tradition of lighting fires on hills. These sacred fires were lit to celebrate the old pagan festival days of Beltane (1 May), Midsummer (21 or 25 June), Hallowe'en and Samhain (31 October and 1 November) and the winter solstice (22 December). These festivals were a relic of ancient sun-worship and are still celebrated today either in local folk-custom or by dedicated people who have revived the pagan spiritual tradition.

Watkins pinpointed beacon hills as one of the most important signs indicating a ley. Not only were the beacons of military use, as in the warning of the coming of the Spanish Armada in 1588, but Watkins had the notion that they had a role in mapping out the ley-line system. He quoted from the Bible to show that the shining light leading the pilgrim along the path was a powerful spiritual metaphor which was also recognized within the religious framework of the ley men.

Crossroads

It was stated earlier that mark stones and wayside crosses were often located at crossroads. The crossing-point of two, three or four roads, tracks or footpaths is considered to be a legitimate ley-marker, although there are some purists who would disagree.

In pagan times, crossroads were venerated because they were sacred to the dark aspect of the goddess who ruled destiny, the underworld, death and rebirth. In ancient Greece crossroads were sacred to both Hermes and the dark goddess Hecate, who was known as 'the goddess of the parting ways'. Anyone who wanted to placate Hecate or request a favour left offerings of food at the place where three roads met. It was believed the goddess could be seen at these crossroads accompanied by the ghosts of the dead and elemental spirits.

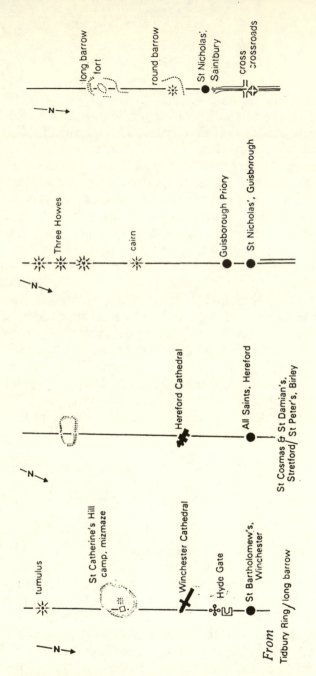

Examples of leys passing through churches and hill-forts

In post-Christian folklore, crossroads were the haunt of ghosts, witches and the Devil. If you wanted to conjure up Old Nick, all you did was visit a crossroad at midnight, sacrifice a black cockerel and call out his name three times. Suicides were buried at crossroads to prevent their souls wandering at night to haunt their relatives. These beliefs are a degenerate folk-memory of the ancient reverence of crossroads as sacred places where mortals could make contact with the Otherworld through pagan religious rituals.

Castles
Medieval castles and manor houses were often constructed on mounds which were settlements in neolithic, Bronze Age and Iron Age periods. When the Normans invaded England in 1066, they initiated a wide-scale programme of castle-building. This construction work was part of their long-term military occupation plan to subdue the indigenous population who had rebelled against the invading Normans.

To save valuable time and to prevent outbreaks of popular uprisings which threatened their rule, the Normans often used existing earthworks to form the foundations of their network of defensive castles. Some of these earthworks dated back to prehistoric times and were ley-markers.

Trees
In pre-Christian times, pagan worshippers, especially the Celts, gathered in sacred groves to worship the Old Gods. As the sites of the worship of the natural powers, these groves were logical markers on ley lines.

Although there are scattered remains of ancient woodland all over the British Isles, many millions of acres of primeval forest have been destroyed by farming and commercial foresting over the centuries since the ley system was established. It is therefore very difficult to find out whether any of the trees we now see in the modern landscape are the descendants of sacred groves. Chanctonbury Ring in Sussex is one obvious contender, even though the present circle of trees is only a few hundred years old, and there are several other copses of trees on hills or earthworks which could have been the sites of sacred groves. However, due to the difficulties of clearly identifying this type of site, most Earth Mysteries researchers tend to overlook trees as authentic ley-markers.

Churches
Many pre-Reformation churches were built on the sites of pagan temples. This was not a coincidence but a deliberate policy instigated by the early Church. When Pope Gregory despatched his Roman missionaries to Britain at the end of the sixth century to convert the heathen Saxons and the pagan Celts, he issued instructions that pagan temples should be changed into places of Christian worship and new churches built on the sites of pagan shrines. He knew the country people regarded these sites as sacred and believed they would be converted more easily if their religious meeting-places were re-dedicated to the new religion.

Churches erected on pagan sites can be recognized, because they often have circular graveyards. These follow the pattern of henges or earthworks which enclosed pagan temples, sacred groves and stone circles. One classic example is Knowlton church in Dorset, whose ruins stand within the centre of a prehistoric earthwork. Local people claim the site has a 'spooky atmosphere', and in recent years it has allegedly been the scene of witchcraft rites.

Many other examples of circular churchyards can be found in Wales, which was Christianized under the influence of the Celtic Church. One of these Welsh churches is St Michael's at Penbryn on the Cardigan coast. It is sometimes described as 'the oldest church in Wales', which is an exaggeration but may indicate its ancient origins in pre-Christian times. The church's present foundations date from the ninth century but there was a wood-and-wattle chapel on the site in the Celtic Christian period.

Penbryn has a circular churchyard but also stands on a prominent mound, providing two pieces of evidence suggesting it was a place of pagan worship. Local folklore claims that the churchyard is circular so that there are no corners for the Devil to hide in. Legend also states that, when a permanent stone building was planned to replace the original chapel, the foundations were laid some miles away. However, the stones laid during the day were mysteriously moved during the night to the present site. The builders heard ethereal voices saying, 'Blessing shall not be thy portion if another site is chosen.' Work was therefore abandoned at the new site and transferred back to the original one on the pagan mound indicated by the ghostly message.

The fact that the church at Penbryn is dedicated to St Michael is of some significance. He was the archangel in Hebrew lore who defeated the rebel angel Lucifer and cast him down to earth. Michael was regarded in Christian mythology as the guardian of the gates of the underworld who protected humankind from the powers of darkness. He was made the patron saint of many churches in the West Country, including the one on Glastonbury Tor, which were originally pagan shrines because of this legendary ability.

Two other churches in West Wales have strong pagan connections which make them ideal examples of ley markers. The first is the ancient church of Nevern in Pembrokeshire, which is dedicated to the Celtic saint Brynach and is only a few miles from the Pentre Ifan cromlech. St Brynach's stands in the shadow of an Iron Age hill-fort which was later used as a Norman castle. According to legend, the Celtic saint spent many years fasting and meditating on a nearby sacred hill called Carn Ingli, where he communicated with angels. In Welsh *Carn Ingli* means 'the hill of the angels'. Inside the churchyard at Nevern is to be found a standing stone carved with the Irish alphabet of Ogham, a fifth-century cross incised with Christian and pagan symbols, and a 'bleeding' yew which is named after the red resin which flows from its trunk.

The other interesting church is St John's at Yspyty Cynfyn, about twelve miles from Aberystwyth. This church dates back to the fifth or sixth century and was deliberately built within a stone circle. Five of the old standing stones, including one which is over ten feet tall, can still be seen embedded in the wall of the churchyard. About two miles away, across a wooded gorge and a river, is a smaller stone circle aligned to the church. The area has medieval associations with the heretical Order of the Knights Templar who, as will be shown later, were guardians of geomantic knowledge from pagan times.

Having established the existence of a ley by finding one or more of the above markers first on a map and then by walking the area, one of the most interesting fields of research is following up any folklore survivals which relate to the alignment. As we have seen, mark stones can be a rich source of folklore material which describe how the stone was moved to its present site by supernatural means. Other legends may relate to attempts to move the stones which resulted in disaster or bad luck for those involved in the enterprise.

Probably the best-known case is that of the barber of Avebury whose remains were excavated from under one of the large standing stones which form the double circle. He had evidently been crushed to death when many of the stones were broken up in the eighteenth century to make walls and foundations for the cottages in the village which now occupies the centre of the circles. There are many other records of people becoming seriously ill, going mad or even dying after attempting to move or break up megalithic monuments. This suggests that the Earth energy operating at these sites can become a negative force if the geomantic siting of the ley-markers is interfered with by humans.

On a more positive level, the power centres on leys are often regarded as healing places. One well-known healing site is the Men-an-Tol complex at Penwith in Cornwall. This consists of a large holed stone flanked by two standing stones. Until fairly recently the central holed stone was used by local people to cure rickets and rheumatism. The afflicted person was passed three times through the hole in the stone to obtain a cure. It is also reputed that in ancient times Stonehenge was used for healing rites. These involved pouring spring water over the stones and then washing in the charged liquid to cure a wide variety of complaints.

References have previously been made to the phallic nature of standing stones, and the shape of stone circles and burial chambers has been equated with the female vagina and the womb. It has been noted earlier that the Pentre Ifan cromlech was known, presumably when it had its original earth mound, as 'the womb of Ceridwen'. Avebury has also been singled out as an example of sexual symbolism carved in stone. The fact that the circle has alternately vertical and lozenge-shaped stones has led to speculation that they are designed to represent the male and female principles believed by the ancients to rule the universe – the God and Goddess of the pagan Old Religion. It is possible that the tradition of 'fertility rites' known to have occurred at ancient sites were originally practised by initiates who used sexual energy for magical purposes.

As an example of what could be described as a typical alignment, the Coldrum ley in Kent provides several of the important factors required for definition, including two churches, a ford, crossed tracks, a pond and a 'holy hill'. The ley is approximately five miles long and begins at Trottiscliffe church, which is curiously pronounced 'Trosley'. This pre-Reformation church is Norman in origin but allegedly had Saxon remains incorporated into its foundations. It has been suggested that the presence of sarsen stones in its vicinity could be the remains of a megalithic circle, but there is no evidence to support this theory. The land on which the church stands was in the eighth century granted to the see of Rochester by King Offa of Mercia and in the eleventh century recorded in the Domesday Book. Inside the church are displayed several items excavated from the nearby Coldrum Stones, a neolithic burial chamber which is another marker on the ley. Local folklore says an underground tunnel leads from the crypt of the church to the Coldrum Stones, which may be a folk-memory of the ley.

The Coldrum Stones are within sight of the church and are

THE COLDRUM LEY

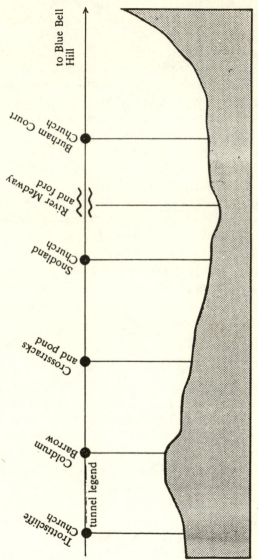

to Blue Bell Hill

Burham Church Court

River Medway and ford

Snodland Church

Crosstracks and pond

Coldrum Barrow

tunnel legend

Trottiscliffe Church

(*The Ley Hunter*)

orientated east–west. Today the site consists of a partly intact burial chamber made of huge stones. The site was investigated in 1910 and over twenty skeletons were unearthed. There is another folk-tradition that hidden treasure is buried under the stones. In recent years the Coldrum Stones have been used as a meeting-place for covens of witches from Kent and South London.

From the Coldrum Stones the ley can be traced to a cross track which has an old pond next to it. A little further on is the village of Snodland, named after a Saxon landowner, which has a pre-Reformation church. From the church can be traced an old pilgrims' path to Canterbury which crossed the nearby river at a ford – now vanished – forming an additional marker.

Across the river is another pre-Reformation church at Burham Court, dedicated to the Virgin Mary, the Christian version of the Great Mother Goddess. Near the church were found the remains of a Roman temple dedicated to the solar god Mithras who was associated with the Zoroastrian fire religion of Persia. The Coldrum ley ends at Bluebell Hill, which has been identified as a sacred hill in pagan times and is aligned to Kit's Coty burial chamber.

Although the maximum length of any one alignment is considered to be twenty miles – and for practical purposes it should be much shorter – some Earth Mysteries researchers claim to have traced leys which greatly exceed this distance. These have been called 'primary leys' which link major sites across the country and can be up to 300 miles long. The existence of these primary leys is a matter of controversy, as not all researchers accept their validity.

Perhaps the most famous of all the primary leys is the so-called Beltane Line which passes through St Michael's Mount in Cornwall, Cadbury Castle in Somerset and Avebury stone circle before ending in Bury St Edmunds in Suffolk, the ancient seat of the Saxon kings. As its name suggests, this alignment allegedly marks the sunrise on 1 May, which was the old Celtic fire festival of Beltane, sacred to the solar god Belinus. The name Beltane means 'the sacred fire of Bel' and

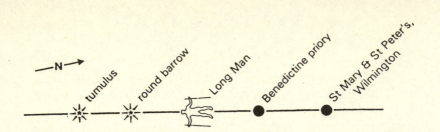

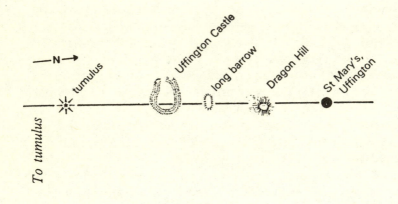

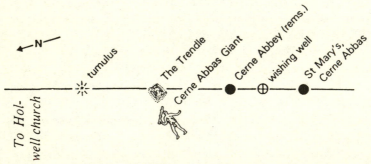

Cerne Abbas, Uffington and Wilmington leys

refers to the druidic custom of driving cattle between two bonfires to protect them magically from disease during the summer season.

Another primary ley allegedly links the Romano-British hill figure of the Cerne Abbas giant with Stonehenge. This ley is allegedly aligned to the midsummer sunrise and passes through several neolithic sites, mounds and beacon hills.

In addition to straight-line alignments, several ley researchers have attempted to link important sacred sites in Britain by triangular alignments. The best-known of these is a large-scale triangle linking the Arbor Low stone circle in Derbyshire with Glastonbury Tor and West Mersea in Essex. Stonehenge is connected in a triangular alignment with Old Sarum and Goreby Castle in the west. Similar primary leys and triangular alignments have also been discovered in France and Germany, suggesting a Europe-wide ley system in prehistoric times.

One particular European site, the village of Alaise in eastern France on the Swiss border, has become the centre of sensational controversy. It has been claimed that the village is the centre point of a series of major primary leys radiating out across Europe. These lines link places as far apart as Alija in Spain, Elsenfeld in Germany, Carlisle in England, Aliso in Corsica, Calais on the French coast and Cales in Italy. The fact that many of the place-names which are linked have similarities with Alaise has led to speculation that in the distant past it was the European centre of an ancient science based on astronomical alignments and the worship of the Goddess. While many of these alignments are very speculative, at least one primary ley which includes several megalithic sites along its path can be traced from Alaise across the Swiss border to Geneva.

As mentioned earlier, when Alfred Watkins wrote about his ley discoveries, he was always aware of their spiritual meaning. While he gave a few broad hints as to their real purpose, he did not expand on these in his written work, and his private thoughts on the subject have gone largely unrecorded. However, modern researchers have followed up his embryonic ideas with startling results, and many now concentrate on the spiritual aspects which they regard as the most important part of Earth Mysteries research.

The most commonly held belief among modern investigators of the ley system from a spiritual angle is that an unknown form of energy flows through the Earth's surface. This energy is concentrated along the ley lines and at the special points, marked by ancient sites, where these alignments cross. It would seem the ancients were fully aware of this invisible web of energy in the landscape and erected their religious monuments at the places where it was most concentrated and potent. Alternatively, a theory has been put forward that, in some way which we cannot as yet understand, the ancient adepts responsible for the ley system created a power network by deliberately placing their sacred sites in a geomantic pattern.

One of the earliest references to this mysterious energy and its connection with sacred power centres in the Western esoteric tradition is to be found in an occult novel written by the late Dion Fortune in the 1930s. In *The Goat Foot God* (William & Norgate, 1936) Fortune has one of her characters refer to 'lines of force' which pass between pre-Christian sites used for pagan sun-worship. These sites are allegedly known to occultists in the fictional context of the novel as 'power centres'. It is further claimed that those who still worship the Old Gods use these lines of force to contact the Unseen or spirit world.

It is known that the shamanic beliefs of the megalithic culture and the Celtic Druids, who inherited their ancient wisdom, were centred on the idea of communication between humans and the extra-terrestrial entities who inhabited the Otherworld. The concept of the power centres as gateways between the material world and other dimensions is frequently to be found in popular folklore. While Fortune may have been influenced by the publication of Watkins' book ten years earlier, her terminology and the fact that she was a practising occultist suggest she had access to esoteric knowledge concerning the use of the ley system and the real purpose of the power centres.

To understand fully the importance given to their sacred sites by the ancients, it is essential to realize that in pre-Christian religions the Earth was often regarded as a living entity represented by a goddess figure. The people who erected the burial mounds, stone circles and standing stones over a period of thousands of years shared a common belief and venerated the life force which they believed created and sustained the universe. This energy manifested as male and female principles which were personified by the archetypal images of the gods and goddesses of pagan mythology.

The idea that the Earth is sacred has received a surprising boost from a new scientific theory which postulates that our planet is a living organism. This controversial theory was put forward in 1972 by Dr James Lovelock of Princeton University, USA, who claims that the Earth is an intelligent entity which regulates the environment in a conscious way. Lovelock called this organic planetary entity Gaia, which was the name of the classical Greek earth goddess.

Although Lovelock has always dismissed the mystical dimension to his theory, many occultists and neo-pagans have accepted it to support their religious beliefs which are centred on the worship of the Great Mother or the Earth goddess. They point out that the Gaian theory of the control of the environment by the planetary entity links with ancient religious rites practised to propitiate the deities believed to be responsible for the growth of vegetation and the weather. These ceremonies were performed at specific festivals timed to coincide with the phases of the moon, the waxing and waning of the sun's power and astronomical events. They were carried out at ancient sites which were often power centres on ley lines, and this has led to a concept of the ley network as the nervous system of Gaia.

At the same time as Dr Lovelock was publishing his thesis on Gaia, students of the Earth Mysteries were attempting to

provide proof that the ley energy existed. The practical skills
of dowsers, psychics and scientists were combined to
investigate ancient sites under the auspices of the Dragon
Project. Dowsers had reported finding energy patterns in the
landscape for many years by using pendulums or dowsing-
rods. They claimed to have found spirals of energy flowing
around standing stones and alleged that the strength of this
energy fluctuated with the phases of the moon. In some cases
this force was so powerful that dowsers working on the stones
were flung backwards. Some dowsers believed that the energy
emanated from the underground streams and subterranean
reservoirs of water which can be found under most ancient
monuments.

While dowsing is still regarded by some people as a suspect
art, the results gained by its use have been confirmed using
more orthodox methods. Using scientific equipment, the
Dragon Project discovered tangible energy effects at stone
circles. The team used ultra-sonic instruments to detect
intensities of energy at the Rollright Stones which coincided
with the dates of the spring and autumn equinoxes – when day
and night are equal – and the winter and summer solstices –
which are the shortest and longest days of the year. Infra-red
photographs of the King Stone clearly show an aura of light
emanating from the top of this monolith.

Further research by the Dragon Project using geiger-
counters has revealed that ancient monuments in Cornwall,
Ireland and Wales have a higher background of radiation than
the surrounding countryside. Other sites were found to have a
very low radiation count, while others deviated between high
and low readings. This has led to the conclusion that stone
circles have a high occurrence of radiation abnormality as
compared with other places in the landscape.

What causes Earth energy and whether it is a natural or
artificial creation remain a mystery at the present time,
although many theories have been put forward to explain it.
We are still a very long way from understanding even the basic
techniques regarding its use which were apparently common

knowledge to our ancestors. It is believed that Earth energy is closely aligned with electro-magnetism and possesses some very odd effects. These include the ability to slow down or stop watches (especially modern time-pieces such as digital watches which use quartz crystals), cause defects in photographic film, disrupt the working of compasses, induce migraine-type headaches in investigators working at sites for long periods, produce sudden and localized changes in temperature, create thunderstorms and manifest psychic phenomena.

Leys and the Earth energy are, of course, not limited to the British Isles but are global phenomena. A brief review of some examples from other countries may offer some clues to the meaning and purpose of Britain' variety.

In the early 1960s a zoologist, writer and film-maker, Tony Morrison, spent several years exploring the Andes region of South America in search of rare types of wildlife. During one of his trips Morrison became fascinated by the enigma of the mysterious Nasca lines which can be found traced across the Peruvian desert. The Nasca alignments are straight lines deliberately carved across the desert plain with uncanny accuracy. Some of the lines extend for over twenty-five miles, and they are accompanied by large drawings, depicting sacred animals, such as the monkey, spider, condor and humming bird. There are also other designs which include flowers and geometric symbols.

Several of the Nasca lines radiate from a central point marked by a small mound of stones. Morrison suggests that the Inca people who once inhabited this area had a belief in *ceques*, 'invisible lines' which radiated out across the countryside and were regarded as spiritually beneficial to the tribes who lived near them. At intervals the lines were marked by a *watka*, a shrine erected to honour a local god. These shrines were in the form of mounds of stones which were used as the site of animal sacrifices. These sacrificial offerings were cremated after their ritual death, and the charred bones were buried under the mound. Archaeologists in Western Europe have found evidence of similar animal cremations buried under megalithic sites which they have been unable to explain.

Morrison became convinced that the Nasca lines had some astronomical meaning, and he discovered that they were aligned to the midwinter and midsummer solstices and to stellar constellations which were mentioned in the myths of the local Indians. Watkins in his later years was also to come to believe that the British ley system had been astronomically aligned by the ancients or, alternatively, that the natural energy flowing through the landscape connected to the cosmic pattern of the night sky.

The alignments which Morrison researched at Nasca were not restricted to South America. In some areas of Texas as late as the 1920s the native Americans crossed hostile countryside by using alignments of stone mounds as markers. In New Mexico archaeologists have discovered a network of alignments dating from prehistoric times. Similar straight-line markers can be found in Mexico and other Central American countries.

An independent investigation of alignments which corresponded to Watkins' leys was carried out by German researchers during the 1930s and 1940s. The playwright and novelist Kurt Gerlach published material during that period on a network of alignments which he claimed criss-crossed northern and central Europe. He plotted straight lines which ran across the German countryside linking castles, monasteries and churches dating from the Middle Ages.

While Watkins was convinced that his old straight tracks were of prehistoric origin, Gerlach believed the German alignments were created by Benedictine monks in the Middle Ages. He claimed the monks used the alignments for communication between the order's religious houses. However, as many of the churches cited by Gerlach were built on pre-Christian sites, it can be safely assumed that the German alignments were also of pagan origin.

The ancient Chinese were also aware of both the Earth

energy and landscape alignments. They called the former 'dragon power', and the lines along which it flowed were 'dragon paths'. In the Chinese philosophy of *feng shui*, which literally means 'wind and water', the Earth was a living entity which had to be respected and revered. They believed the planet and the universe were activated by spiritual energy known as *chi*, which can manifest in either a *yin*, or feminine aspect, or a *yang*, or masculine form. The female force flows along the hills and the male along the valleys. However, sometimes these roles are reversed and the female is known as 'the spirit of the valley', which is a coded reference to the female vagina as a source of healing energy which is beneficial to the male during sexual intercourse.

The geomancers who practise the cult of *feng shui* were employed by wealthy families to choose sites for houses or burial places. This practice was to ensure that their occupants, living or dead, could take full advantage of the revitalizing properties of the positive currents of the dragon power. The life force or *chi* flows through the rocks of the Earth like water. It can change character when it encounters geographical features which obstruct its progress. These changes can adversely effect the nature of the Earth energy, creating a malefic force which in the West is known as a 'black ley'.

Because the ancient Chinese were ancestor-worshippers, they believed that the good luck or fortune bestowed on mortals by the gods could be affected by their relationship with dead relatives. If the tombs of the deceased were not correctly aligned geomantically to take advantage of the positive flow of the dragon power, great misfortune would be visited upon the family concerned. In such cases a geomancer was hired to find the best site for the tomb in accordance with geomantic conditions. If the correct place was not found, the spirits of the dead could return to haunt the living and might even develop vampiric tendencies.

Stone circles, cromlechs and standing stones can be found all over the world, in places as wide apart as the United States, India, West Africa, Japan and the Middle East. The

knowledge of the ley lines and Earth energies was well known
in ancient times, linking Europe, Africa, Asia and the
Americas culturally. This fact suggests that in some distant
historical period a universal belief-system once existed. This
ancient wisdom recognized the sacredness of the land,
venerated the Earth as a goddess and used the dragon power
for magical and spiritual purposes.

2
ASTRO-ARCHAEOLOGY

The system of alignments known popularly as ley lines which link megalithic sites and the existence of the Earth energy has been incorporated into the new science of astro-archaeology. This subject is attracting more and more support from Earth Mysteries researchers as a possible explanation for the ley system. As its name suggests, astro-archaeology is a fusing of the study of archaeology with astronomy to provide the theory that the ancient sites were deliberately aligned to calendar events and astronomical phenomena.

Even before the megalithic builders erected the stone circles, the ancients seem to have had a sophisticated knowledge of astronomy. In both cave paintings and stone or bone artefacts the early hunter-gatherers of the Ice Age period have left evidence which reveals their astronomical knowledge. The paleolithic (Old Stone Age) skywatchers used ritual batons or wands made from reindeer bones to record stellar activity, and remains of these objects have been found in their cave dwellings.

At first archaeologists dismissed the lines carved on these objects as 'hunting marks', but it was discovered that in fact they were a crude but effective record of the monthly movements of the moon and its changing phases. It has now been accepted that these ritual batons were an early attempt by prehistoric astronomers to create a calendar measuring the passage of time by observing the lunar phases.

Many thousands of years before the megalithic culture, this type of lunar observation had been established as an integral part of early religious ideas concerning the cosmos and humankind's role in it. The early humans used this astronomical knowledge initially for timing-hunting rituals but later, as agricultural techniques developed, they charted the progress of the sun and the moon to measure the progression of the seasons.

An examination of early religious practices indicates that sun-, moon- and star-worship was a feature of early human cultures. Stellar worship was centred on the spiritual significance of important constellations including the Great Bear (Ursa major) and the North (Pole) Star. The latter was regarded by the ancients as the centre of the universe around which all the other constellations were believed to revolve. Symbolically, the Pole Star was the pivot of the universe, and in Northern European myth it was the focal point of the cosmic Tree of Life. Our modern practice of placing a star on the top of the traditional Christmas tree ultimately derives from this pagan belief.

It was in the observation of the night sky for religious purposes, which was later to develop into astrology, that the development of astronomy reached its highest point. The Sumerians and Babylonians, for instance, were aware of the movements of the stars, the phases of the moon and the solstices and equinoxes. They could also predict lunar and solar eclipses with some accuracy. The stellar religion of Babylonia and Chaldea revolved around the worship of the goddess of love and war, Ishtar, and the veneration of the planet Venus, the so-called morning and evening star, as her symbol in the sky.

In the sophisticated Babylonian study of stellar phenomena for religious purposes can be discerned the abilities of the prehistoric astronomers who preceded them and used the megalithic circles as calendars. Why were these early astronomer priests so fascinated by the mysteries of the night sky? One theory which has been put forward is that the early human cultures were in contact with the extra-terrestrials who originated from the star systems they studied. Other theories claim that the first humans, who operated on a more intuitive level than modern homo sapiens, were sensitive to the cosmic influences which emanated from the stars and formed the basis of astrology.

The actual study of astro-archaeology within Earth Mysteries is only of comparatively recent origin. Some of the early pioneers of the subject had formulated the theory but it was not until our own century that astro-archaeology became an essential aspect of Earth Mysteries research. The first person who is credited with introducing the idea in its sophisticated form in historical times was an eighteenth-century architect, John Wood. He made a careful study of Stonehenge and the impressive stone circle of Stanton Drew outside Bristol and decided that both sites were the product of astronomical knowledge from ancient times.

It was Wood's opinion that the whole area of southern England around Stonehenge and Avebury was sacred to the ancients. Wood lived in Bath and believed that the seven hills on which the city had been built represented the seven classical planets: the sun, moon, Mercury, Mars, Jupiter, Venus and Saturn. Bath in Roman times was the site of a temple to the Greek solar god Apollo, who was a deity of healing. The city has also been found to be the cult centre in Celtic times of the goddess Sulis Minerva, who was worshipped at a sacred spring.

According to Wood, the nearby Wookey Hole (an underground cave which was once the home of a local witch), Silbury Hill, Avebury and Stonehenge had all been major sites of druidic worship in the area. He spent a considerable time at each of the sites, surveying them with measuring-rods before reaching any conclusions about their prehistoric use. Wood's theories were, of course, heavily influenced by the eighteenth-

and nineteenth-century belief that the stone monuments of the megalithic period had been erected by the Celtic Druids. Today the latest archaeological findings suggest that a proto-druidic religion existed in Western Europe predating the development of the Celts as a separate racial entity around 1,000 BCE. It is therefore possible that the eighteenth- and nineteenth-century antiquarians who claimed the Druids used megalithic sites were not completely mistaken in their belief.

When Wood published his first findings on Stonehenge in 1740, he stated that the circle was astronomically aligned. It was used, according to Wood, by the Druids as a cosmic calendar. He regarded the stones in the circle as symbolic representations of the lunar months of the year, the number of days in a decade and the lunar phases. This information was allegedly used by the Druids to calculate the dates of their religious festivals.

It is an interesting fact, considering the strange nature of the Earth energy at megalithic sites and ley centres, that, when Wood visited Stonehenge and Stanton Drew, fierce thunderstorms began the moment he produced his measuring-rods! At Stonehenge the severity of the storm forced him to abandon his survey and seek refuge in a cottage which had been built near the stone circle.

John Wood's researches were followed up by others who became interested in astronomical alignments as a result of his work in the field. One of these was Dr John Smith who, writing in the latter half of the eighteenth century, claimed that the famous Heel Stone, which can be found at Stonehenge, was a marker for the midsummer sunrise. He speculated that the original number of monoliths in the outer circle at Stonehenge, if multiplied by twelve, the number of the signs of the Zodiac, produced the 360 days of the solar year. The inner circle he claimed represented the monthly lunar cycle of approximately twenty-nine days. He felt that these facts, taken together, suggested that Druids (or the megalith-builders) used Stonehenge as a temple to worship the sun and the moon.

Because Stonehenge stands in an isolated position on Salisbury Plain, commands a panoramic view over the surrounding countryside and has a high visibility of the open sky, many of the early researchers found it easy to accept that its original use was as an astronomical observatory and calendar. It was presumed that the Druids used it and other megalithic monuments by combining astronomical and astrological knowledge in religious ceremonies based on the monthly cycle of the moon and the annual solar cycle.

Contemporary with Wood was an antiquarian cleric, Dr William Stukeley, who was also interested in the ancient sites. He was a Church of England clergyman who was also the leader at one period of the neo-Celtic revival of the eighteenth century. This revival began in 1717 with the re-forming of the Druid Order on the autumn equinox at Primrose Hill in London. As well as having an interest in druidism, Stukeley devoted his time to studying Avebury, the nearby Silbury Hill and the West Kennet long barrow.

Stukeley was the grand master of the Society of Roman Knights, a small group of men and women who travelled all over Britain examining and recording ancient monuments. It was in his position as the leader of this group that he investigated the Avebury complex and Stonehenge. The results of this work were published in two volumes, entitled *Stonehenge: A Temple Restored to the British Druids* (1740) and *Avebury: A Temple of the British Druids* (1743).

In Stukeley's book, Avebury is depicted in an illustration as a double circle of standing stones enclosed within a larger circle of monoliths. He shows the avenue of stones leading to and from Avebury as a serpentine structure snaking across the landscape and through the main circle which today stands within the medieval village. Some observers have seen this serpent at Avebury as a symbol of the dragon power flowing from the circle and have regarded Stukeley as an initiate who was aware of the esoteric uses of Earth energy. Stukeley himself appears to have regarded the Avebury serpent as a symbol of the 'true faith', i.e. Christianity, which pre-dated the birth of the Christ. He considered the serpent a legitimate symbol of God, although it appears to be a heretical image which has more in common with Gnosticism than orthodox Christian belief. The cleric was on surer ground when he declared the serpent was a symbol of the universal religion which was practised here before the coming of Christianity.

The extensive removal of the stones from the Avebury circle in historical times has made it very difficult to imagine how the site looked originally. It is possible that Stukeley's vision of the site as two twin circles may not be correct. In 1988 two seventeenth-century plans of Avebury were rediscovered in the archives of the Royal Society in London which provide a different perspective. The first map was drawn by John Aubrey between 1648 and 1663 and shows four concentric circles enclosed within a larger earthwork. A second map, drawn in 1663 by Dr Walter Charleton, physician to King Charles II, shows only one circle, with a smaller stone circle in its south-east quadrant. Both maps indicate the presence of stones outside the earthwork arranged at each quarter. This has led to speculation that originally there were four avenues of stones leading from the main Avebury circle towards the cardinal points of the compass. This suggests that originally Avebury was in the form of a Celtic cross, with the main circle at its centre. This 'Celtic cross' is a feminine symbol which can also be found in the design of many prehistoric burial chambers and represents the vagina and womb of the Great Mother Goddess.

Stukeley's major contribution to early astro-archaeology was his theory that the axis of Stonehenge, together with the avenue which led up to it, was orientated towards the midsummer sunrise. The cleric knew that the Druids practised astronomy, as this fact was recorded by classical writers who had encountered their religion. He took this to its logical conclusion in his own study of the henge. His view was taken up by Dr John Smith in 1770 when he declared that Stonehenge had been a druidic temple for observing the stars.

Today we know that Stonehenge was not built by the Celts but was erected in several phases over a period of several hundred years around 4,000 years ago. However, the proposition that megalithic monuments were used as astronomical purposes remained only one of many, often bizarre, theories about these ancient remains. It was not until the early 1900s that the idea was explored in any depth and firm evidence put forward to support its validity.

It was the work of the scientist Sir Norman Lockyer which was firmly to establish astro-archaeology as a serious subject for study. It was Lockyer who first coined the evocative term 'astronomer priests' which is widely used today to describe the ancient architects who were responsible for the stone circles. Lockyer was a well-known astronomer, a fellow of the Royal Society and the director of the solar physics laboratory in South Kensington, London. In 1890 he visited Greece and was surprised to discover that many of the Greek temples were orientated to the sunrise. This discovery led him to travel to Egypt, where he carried out a survey of temples in relation to their possible alignment to the sunrise and sunset.

The astronomer's researches at Karnak in Egypt showed that the temple dedicated to the solar god Amon-Ra was built so that it was orientated to sunset on the summer solstice. Lockyer calculated that in 3,700 BCE the rays of the sun as it set over the Egyptian desert would have entered the temple's inner sanctum. The rays travelled along a corridor which gradually narrowed downwards. This astronomical event is paralleled by the beam of sunlight which enters the Newgrange burial mound in Ireland at sunrise on the winter solstice.

In addition to this discovery, Lockyer also calculated that several other Egyptian temples were aligned to the rising and setting of stars in the vicinity of the north and south poles. This led him to think that the temples might have been used by the Ancient Egyptians as astronomical clocks. Other temples he found were orientated towards the star Sirius, worshipped as a form of the goddess Isis by the Egyptians because its rising coincided with the flooding of the Nile delta which fertilized the fields.

In Egyptian mythology Sirius was known as the Dog Star
and was also identified with the dark god Set who in the later
period of Egyptian history was regarded as the personification
of evil. Set was known as the Lord of the Desert and in myth
was the opponent of Osiris, the god of vegetation. The linking
of Set with the star Sirius suggests that the dark god was
originally a deity who may have been a product of a chthonic
cult of stellar worship.

When he had completed his studies of the Egyptian
temples, Lockyer returned to Britain and turned his attentions
to the sacred sites there. He began by conducting an
investigation of Stonehenge which culminated in 1906 in the
publication of his book *Stonehenge and Other British Stone
Monuments Astronomically Calculated*, which caused a sensa-
tion in archaeological circles. In this book he put forward the
idea that many of Britain's stone circles were aligned to the
sun and major stars, whose spiritual meaning was part of the
mythology of the peoples who had erected the monuments.

Lockyer identified these people as a pre-Celtic race who had
colonized the British Isles from the east. It was his opinion
that the Druids inherited the wisdom of these early astronomer
priests, but he stated that the Celts had not erected the
megalithic monuments. He further believed that the fire
festivals practised by the Celtic tribes – Beltane (1 May),
Lughnasadh (1 August), Samhain (1 November) and Imbolc
(1 February) – had also been inherited from the megalithic
culture. These festivals, together with the solstices and the
equinoxes, divided the year into eight parts based on the solar
cycle. This ritual pattern can be found in Celtic, Germanic and
Norse versions of the pagan Old Religion.

Lockyer's book suggested that in ancient times Stonehenge
was a temple used for sun-worship and was aligned to sunrise
and sunset on the quarter days, which became the Celtic fire
festivals. In a later stage of its use, the astronomical
alignments were abandoned by the people using the henge,
although they still celebrated important festivals on the
solstices and the equinoxes.

One of the interesting results of Lockyer's research was his discovery that the astronomical alignments at Stonehenge could be extended beyond the circle into the countryside around it. In fact, the lines traced from the henge extend as far away as Silbury Hill, according to Lockyer.

It seems Lockyer's alignments have something in common with Alfred Watkins' leys (re)discovered in the 1920s. Watkins was certainly influenced by the astronomer, for he uses the results of Lockyer's research in his own works to support the existence of the ley system. In Watkins' second book, *The Ley Hunter's Manual*, published in 1927, he specifically refers to the work by Lockyer in relation to the survival of ancient sun-worship in modern folk-customs.

Watkins mentions the old Wiltshire custom of visiting Stonehenge on Midsummer Day (the summer solstice?) to see the sun rise down the avenue which leads to the circle. This practice was carried out for generations before the modern Druids were granted permission to hold their solstice ceremony at the stones in 1904. In his book Watkins goes on to mention several other astronomical alignments at hills and churches where the orientation is to the sunrise on significant pagan dates such as May Day and Midsummer.

Finally, Watkins supports Lockyer's belief that the ancient wisdom of the astronomer priests was passed on to the Celts and others who followed in their mystical footsteps. In *The Old Straight Track* he says: '... I feel that the ley man, astronomer priest, druid, bard, wizard, witch, palmer and hermit were all more or less linked by one thread of ancient knowledge and power, however degenerate it became in the end....' He qualified this statement by saying that, although he was convinced of its truth, he could offer no genealogy to support its conclusion.

As could be expected, Lockyer's research into the astronomical alignments of ancient sites was greeted with scepticism and in some cases derision by the archaeological establishment. His insistence that the stone circles were not a product of druidism was also attacked by those who were involved in the Celtic Revival. They chose to ignore Lockyer's belief that the Druids had inherited a corpus of arcane knowledge from the megalith-builders and that fragments of this had survived in the existing bardic circles of Wales, Cornwall and Brittany. Lockyer had visited several of the ancient sites in West and North Wales, especially those on Yns Mon (Anglesey). He was also aware of the bardic tradition and its revival which had taken place in the eighteenth century under the influence of the neo-Druid Iolo Morganwg (aka Edward Williams). This politically radical Welsh bard had drawn up plans for a traditional *gorsedd* circle to be used by modern Druids which incorporated astronomical alignments.

Morganwg's plan for the stone circle includes several stones arranged outside it which were aligned to the sunrise at the solstices and equinoxes. Lockyer was convinced the Welsh bard had access to pre-Celtic knowledge when he drew up the plans for the *gorsedd* circle. When Lockyer began to survey some of the Cornish stone circles, he found confirmation of this belief. The Boscawen-un circle was aligned to sunrise at the summer solstice and at the Celtic festivals of Beltane and Samhain.

Other researchers began to follow up Lockyer's work, and some began field studies on the Isle of Lewis in the Hebrides to investigate the impressive megalithic circle of Callanish for evidence of astronomical alignments. The stones of Callanish are situated on a ridge which provides the observer with a magnificent view of the nearby Loch Roag and the mountains of Harris. They form part of a vast prehistoric religious complex which includes seven other stone circles in the immediate area. Although today the Isle of Lewis is a cold, bleak place, when Callanish was built Britain in general was enjoying an almost sub-tropical climate.

In common with the newly discovered layout of Avebury, the Callanish circle was laid out in the shape of a Celtic cross. It measures 405 feet from north to south and 140 feet from west to east. In the centre is a circle of thirteen standing stones, ranging from eight to twelve feet high, which is forty-two feet in diameter. Inside the circle are the remains of a burial mound which in prehistoric times was the scene of a ritual cremation. To the west and east of the circle are four more standing stones on each side. To the south extends a double row of nineteen stones, forming a ceremonial avenue leading to the main circle.

As with Stonehenge, numerous theories have been suggested to explain the siting of this impressive religious centre on a remote Scottish island. These theories have included the claim that the stone circle was a temple to Apollo erected by Greek travellers, that it was a sacred place of dragon- or serpent-worship, the burial place of a semi-mythical king or a beacon built by ancient astronauts to guide UFOs.

Apart from these theories put forward by outsiders, there are several local legends which allegedly explain the existence of the stones. One states that the stones were brought to the island thousands of years ago by a priest king from a distant land across the sea. (Atlantis?) The king was accompanied by a group of black men who erected the circle under his directions. The priest king wore a cloak of brightly coloured feathers and always appeared with wrens flying around him.

In 1680 a written description of the Isle of Lewis includes a reference to a folktale that the Callanish circle comprised men who were transformed into stone by an enchanter. In the seventeenth century the circle was known locally as *Fir Bhreige*, which is the Gaelic for 'the false men'. The belief that stone circles and standing stones were the petrified remains of humans who had been bewitched or turned into stone by God for committing some terrible sin – such as dancing on the Sabbath – was a common one in the Middle Ages.

Callanish was also called the *Fursachan*, a Gaelic word translated as 'the place of pilgrimage', and this may be a reference to its original religious use. The word Callanish itself comes from the Old Norse *Kjallirs Ness*. Kjallir was an old name for Odin, the one-eyed shaman god of Northern European mythology, and Ness is a headland or promontory.

It is known that the Vikings visited the Scottish isles, and the circle's name dates from that period.

As late as the nineteenth century certain families on the Isle of Lewis were popularly believed to be hereditary guardians of the stones, and this tradition survives today. This was a task which had been handed down through generations from the earliest times. The local clergy had forbidden anyone to visit the circle on the dates of the old pagan festivals. However, these families ignored this edict and still went to the site in secret, because they believed the stones should never be neglected.

In local folklore, sunrise on the summer solstice (21 June) heralded the arrival of a mysterious presence known as 'The Shining One'. The arrival of this supernatural personage was marked by the call of a cuckoo. This may account for the widely held belief that each cuckoo which arrives on the island in the spring flies straight to the stones to give its first call. A similar tradition can be found in Wales, where cuckoos traditionally fly first to the Celtic cross in the graveyard of St Brynach's Church in Pembrokeshire.

In the late seventeenth century the historical chronicler Martin Martin gave the first account of Callanish in his book *A Description of the Western Islands of Scotland*, published in 1695. He mentions that local people believed the circle had been used for druidic worship in the past and that the Chief Druid had stood in the centre of the circle and preached to his congregation. As late as the early 1900s quasi-druidic ceremonies were held at the stones. These involved the extinguishing of all fires on the island on Beltane (May Day) and the relighting of them from a sacred fire which blazed in the centre of the circle.

When he visited the Western Isles, Martin Martin also surveyed the Stones of Stenness and the Ring of Brodgar on the Orkneys. He regarded Stenness as having been a temple of the moon, and Brodgar as a place dedicated to sun-worship. John Toland, who was one of those responsible for the revival of Druidism in 1717, was convinced that both Callanish and the Orkney circles had been druidic temples. He further claimed that Callanish had been a temple for the worship of the sun and the moon. In 1808 Thomas Headrick visited the circle and said afterwards that it had been planned as a cross to indicate the four cardinal points and the rising of the sun, moon and various stars. He saw the place as an astronomical calendar which marked the seasons of the year and the hours of the day. Another nineteenth-century investigator, Donald Wilson, writing some fifty years later, supported Headrick and claimed Callanish as 'a memorial to primitive astronomy'.

Modern examinaton of the Callanish stone circle has confirmed that it was designed to be both a lunar and a solar observatory. Lockyer never went to the site himself but he worked on plans of the site which convinced him that the avenue of stones leading south from the circle were aligned to the star Capella in 1720 BCE. He also plotted a second alignment from the remains of the central burial mound which marked the rise of the Pleiades or Seven Sisters constellation as viewed by an observer inside the circle in 1330 BCE.

Between 1908 and 1912 the surveyor, hydrographer and naval officer Rear-Admiral Boyle Somerville conducted a survey of ancient monuments in Scotland, including Callanish. He subsequently published his findings in the academic journal *Archaeologia*, stating that the avenue, the west and east rows and several stones in the circle were astronomically aligned. Somerville found separate alignments to the rising of Capella and the Pleiades, as well as to sunset at the equinoxes and full moonrise at the winter solstice.

Other alignments found at Callanish reveal that it is orientated towards major solar events during the year. These include the sunrise and sunset points of the summer solstice, sunset and sunrise at the spring and autumn equinoxes (21 March and 22 September) and sunset and sunrise on the winter solstice. Somerville's survey also indicated the existence of lunar alignments based on the moon's monthly cycle. The admiral believed Callanish had been chosen by the astronomer priests as a lunar temple because of its unique position for observing the moon. For a few days every eighteen years, the moon rises so close to due south at this latitude that its path across the sky is less than two degrees above the horizon. To an observer standing in the circle, the moon appears to skim the mountain skyline, which some researchers have seen as the outline of a naked woman – the Earth goddess – in the Scottish landscape.

This unusual lunar phenomenon at Callanish may have led to the supposition that the stone circle was a temple to Apollo, as described by the Greek writer Diodorus in 55 BCE. He wrote about a mysterious, mist-shrouded island which was the home of the legendary Hyperboreans or 'dwellers beyond the north wind':

Opposite to the coast of Celtic Gaul there is an island in the ocean, not smaller than Sicily, lying to the north, which is inhabited by the Hyperboreans who are so named because they dwell beyond the north wind. Tradition says that Leto, the mother of Apollo, was born there and for this reason the inhabitants venerate Apollo more than any other god. In island there is a magnificent precinct of Apollo and a remarkable temple in a round form adorned with many consecrated gifts. There is also a city sacred to the same god most of the inhabitants of which are harpers.

The Hyperboreans have a peculiar dialect and have a remarkable attachment to the Greeks, especially to the Athenians and the Delians deducing their friendship from remote periods. It is related that some Greeks visited the Hyperboreans with whom they left great consecrated gifts of value and also that Aboris, coming from the Hyperboreans into Greece, renewed their family intercourse with Greece and the Delians.

It is also said that in this land the moon appears very close to the Earth, so near that certain eminences of a terrestrial form can be plainly seen on it. Apollo visits this island once in a course of 19 years in which period the stars complete their revolutions and for that reason the Greeks distinguish the cycle of 19 years by the name of 'The Great Year'. During the season of his appearance the god plays upon his harp and dances through from the vernal equinox to the rising of the Pleiades.

The clues which connect this almost mythical island of the Hyperboreans with the Isle of Lewis were fervently followed up by the early researchers who were investigating the island's stone circles. They pointed out that 'the round temple' could refer to Callanish and that 'the city', in Greek terms could be a description of a large Bronze Age settlement near the circle. The fact that the moon does appear very near to the Earth and that the solar god worshipped by the Hyperboreans, identified by the Greek writer with his native deity Apollo, visited the island every nineteen years also points to the area around Callanish. References to the vernal equinox and the Pleiades in this respect could also indicate the astronomical alignments at the stone circle. Apollo's mother, Leto, was associated with the Pleiades and had a daughter, Diana, who was a huntress goddess of the moon.

It is interesting that the account of the Hyperboreans mentions Aboris, who is described as the high priest of the temple of Apollo. It seems that Aboris was either born in Hyperborea or visited it as a messenger between its inhabitants and the ancient Greeks. Aboris shares his name with the teacher of the Greek philosopher Pythagoras, and Pythagorean right-angled triangles were used in megalithic circle design thousands of years before they were allegedly invented in Greece.

The stellar alignments at Callanish where challenged by orthodox archaeologists who were reluctant to accept their authenticity. However, in the 1960s an American astronomer, Professor Gerald Hawkins, used a computer to confirm the existence of the alignments relating to the lunar and solar points. Hawkins believed that the astronomer priests had used Callanish as a primitive computer to calculate a calendar based on the lunar phases. The number of months in a lunar year, thirteen, coincided with the number of standing stones in the circle. The nineteen stones in the avenue related to the lunar cycle of the 'moon standstill' which can be observed from Callanish. Whatever the truth about the alignment of Callanish to the stars, the fact that it was a temple of the sun and the moon seems to be beyond any doubt.

One of the major contributions to astro-archaeology in recent years has been the work of the late Professor Alexander Thom, a retired professor of engineering at Oxford University who spent many years surveying and measuring megalithic sites all over Britain. His findings were published in three important books, *Megalithic Sites in Britain* (1967), *Megalithic Lunar Observatories* (1971) and *Megalithic Remains in Britain and Brittany* (1979). Although Thom was criticized by orthodox archaeologists, probably because he was a gifted amateur who dared to intrude into their hallowed profession, his research into the megalithic mystery has been regarded by those with more open minds as a valuable addition to our understanding of prehistoric society and religion.

Thom followed on from the work of earlier pioneers such as Lockyer and Somerville. He had read the admiral's research notes on Callanish in 1912 while still a young man, and this had triggered his interest in the ancient sites. In 1930 Thom visited Callanish by accident for, while he was sailing in the area, bad weather forced him ashore on the Isle of Lewis. He went to the stones and observed that the Pole Star was in alignment with the circle. It was this observation that was later to lead him to conclude that the ancients used stone circles for astronomical observation as calendars.

While he followed in the footsteps of the earlier researchers, Thom's engineering background made him analyse the sites in a more precise way than those who had preceded him. Several years of concentrated work convinced him that the megalith-builders were highly skilled in geometric calculation and astronomical observation. He came to believe that the prehistoric society responsible for the stone circles was sophisticated and possessed knowledge which we have lost today. Indeed, it was this belief which was to lead to a radical reappraisal of the megalithic culture by many enlightened archaeologists and historians.

One of Thom's innovative contributions to our understanding of how the stone circles were constructed was his discovery of the so-called 'megalithic yard'. This was a standard unit of measurement of approximately 2.72 feet, which he claimed had been employed by the megalith-builders to measure out their circles. The use of the word 'yard' was deliberate, because Thom thought this word derived from a wooden measuring-rod called a yardstick used by the ancients in circle-building.

It was Thom's firm conviction that in the distant past, when orthodox archaeology claimed humans were primitive savages, there existed a centralized organization or source of technical knowledge which was the impetus behind the design and construction of the stone circle network. This knowledge was based on astronomical observation, for he concluded that the astronomer priests used distant mountain peaks or 'notches' between hills in conjunction with standing stones in the landscape to measure accurately the movement of the moon. By using this method of observation, the priests could predict lunar eclipses for a religious purpose.

It is interesting that in the 1920s Alfred Watkins had described landscape notches as potential sighting-points. Investigations carried out by Watkins in the Black Mountains of Wales had revealed the existence of several of these notches which marked the passage of alignments across the Welsh countryside.

Professor Thom accepted that the neolithic and Bronze Age people who set up the stone circles had attained a high level of mathematical expertise and engineering skill. This had been achieved without recourse to written textbooks, either by trial and error or by intuition or perhaps through a combination of the two. Thom was the first researcher to identify the use of the 'Pythagorean' right-angled triangle in the measurement of many stone circles at least 2,000 years before it was known in Greece. He further discovered that not all the circles were perfect in shape but that many were ovoid or egg shaped. This shape had been deliberately calculated by the megalith-builders so they could adjust their measurements for mathematical reasons.

Whatever the orthodox view of these ancient people, Thom's evaluation of their monuments presented them as practitioners of a sophisticated form of technology. However, unlike modern technology, the megalithic version was intimately interwoven with a religious belief which embraced a holistic vision of the universe.

Conventional theories about the purpose of the stone circles was further challenged in 1963, when Professor Gerald Hawkins of Boston University offered the scientific community the fruits of his computerized research into megalithic alignments. He published the full results of his investigations in his book *Stonehenge Decoded* (1965), which became an international bestseller. In the 1950s Hawkins had worked at a missile-testing base on Salisbury Plain, about a mile from Stonehenge. During his period of service at the base he had spent a considerable amount of his spare time visiting the henge and exploring the barrows around it. Hawkins had been trained as an astronomer, and he knew that the modern Druids visited the circle at dawn on the summer solstice to witness the sunrise. This fact led him to speculate about this particular alignment and to wonder if there were any others to be discovered at the site.

It was not until 1960 that Hawkins was able to return to Salisbury Plain and investigate the Stonehenge alignments in earnest. He began his task by visiting the stones on the morning of the summer solstice, when the sun appears to rise over the Heel Stone as viewed from inside the circle. From this visit germinated Hawkins' mission to discover, using the latest scientific methods, if other solar alignments existed at the site. He was also interested in finding out if there were alignments centred on the moon and the stars at the circle.

As with Thom's researches, Hawkins was following lines of investigation carried out earlier by people such as Sir Norman Lockyer. In 1906 Lockyer had attempted to establish a firm date for the construction of Stonehenge and had surveyed it for evidence of astronomical alignments. He had concluded that Stonehenge was aligned to the midsummer sunrise, producing evidence which confirmed the findings of the Rev. Edward Duke, who, writing in the nineteenth century, had decided that the circle and its adjacent monuments were part of a gigantic model of the solar system mapped out in the Wiltshire landscape. Hawkins wanted to prove the astronomical alignments by a scientific method which could not be disputed by sceptical archaeologists.

In this respect Hawkins was far more successful than Lockyer, for he estimated that the possibility existed at Stonehenge of over 27,000 separate alignments between 165 positions. He also estimated that lines extended from any one of these positions were likely to point to some object in the sky. Faced with this wealth of information, Hawkins used a computer to calculate which of these many alignments were the important ones. Data on the 165 positions and their possible alignments were fed into the computer. In less then sixty seconds Hawkins was provided with 240 major alignments which were connected to celestial declinations.

Having established this fact, Hawkins wanted to know if the points where the important Stonehenge alignments 'hit' the night sky were special in any way; for example, did they mark the rising- or setting-points of stellar objects? The raw data provided by the computer gave Hawkins a mass of information which was riddled with a large number of duplications. He decided to concentrate on these, and by a slow process of elimination he found that the declinations the computer had isolated pointed – quite literally – to the movements of the sun and the moon.

The information Hawkins had used to programme the computer was based on very crude approximations of the sun and the moon in the night sky at the period when Stonehenge was being used as a religious centre, around 2,000 BCE. More accurate data was given to the computer, which processed it to reveal that in megalithic times there was no question that the stones had been aligned to the passage of the sun and the moon across the sky at different times of the year. The computer had discovered no fewer than twelve of the major alignments of

Stonehenge pointing to an extreme position of the sun to a mean accuracy of less than one degree. A further twelve alignments pointed to the extreme position of the moon and had a mean accuracy of 1½ degrees.

Hawkins pointed out that, when the modern Druids gather to greet the solstice dawn, a six-foot-tall person who views the sun rising while standing in the centre of the circle will see that the top of the Heel Stone is level with the skyline in the distance. In 1800 BCE a person standing in that exact position would have seen the sun rise about three-quarters of a degree to the left of the top of the Heel Stone. The lower edge of the sun would therefore have passed half a degree above the stone, if it had been leaning at the same angle it is today. Hawkins was convinced the stone was upright in 1800 BCE and that the sun would have just touched the top of it as it rose in the dawn sky. The priests and the congregation would therefore have witnessed the rising disc of the sun 'rest' on top of the stone marker as it rose.

Hawkins' calculations suggested that Stonehenge had been solar-orientated and was a religious centre for sun-worship in prehistoric times. This view was slightly amended by further discoveries made by Alexander Thom, C.A. Newham and Hawkins himself which gave the moon a religious prominence at the site as well. In addition to the midsummer sunrise and midwinter sunset alignments at the circle, there were also the twelve moon alignments which prove that Stonehenge was used as a lunar observatory.

Despite the fact that the construction of Stonehenge took place over several centuries, these findings suggest that the lunar and solar alignments were never lost. This indicates that the period during which the various phases of the henge were built was a stable and peaceful one. The building of the henge and the ritual use of the site must have been carried out without any fear of social upheaval or outside interference.

The fact that the knowledge of the midsummer sunrise and the other alignments was preserved without the aid, as far as we know, of a written alphabet is evidence of an oral tradition passed down through generations of megalithic architects and priests. By modern standards this is a remarkable achievement which alone completely refutes the popular image of the prehistoric inhabitants of ancient Europe as primitive and brutish savages.

Recent archaeological discoveries, dating back before the megalithic period, suggest that early humankind was far more developed than previously believed. An excavation in Suffolk, for instance, has uncovered flint tools at least 500,000 years old, which pre-date the Ice Age. A British Museum expert said, 'This find throws conventional ideas about cultural succession completely out of the window.'

In Yugoslavia an American anthropologist studying 60,000-year-old human remains discovered evidence which corrects previously held misconceptions about the Neanderthals. He claims that, far from being the savage beasts of popular lore, the Neanderthal people were caring types who had basic medical knowledge and techniques for tending the sick, wore clothes made of animal skins, used fire for cooking, had stone tools, possessed religious concepts and even used toothpicks to clean their teeth after meals!

Evidence of early Bronze Age mines dug 1,500 years before the Romans were believed to have originated mining have also been discovered in Wales, adding to the belief that the megalithic culture was not unique but was part of an ongoing pattern of advanced human development spanning many thousands of years.

While modern researchers, approaching the subject from a scientific angle, have revealed the extent to which the ancients used stone circles for the observation of astronomical phenomena, they have generally not offered any specific reason for this practice in prehistoric times. Any attempt fully to understand why a vast network of lunar, solar and stellar observatories was set up across the planet in prehistory must take into consideration the spiritual beliefs of the megalith-builders in so far as these can be ascertained.

The official noticeboards erected by English Heritage or the Department of the Environment at stone circles they administer state that the monuments were erected 'for some religious purpose'. Unfortunately, from the available fragmented archaeological records it is not always possible to define exactly what type of religion the megalithic people practised. However, it is not too difficult to make some educated guesses based on the folklore associated with sacred places and the pattern of religious development which has descended from the megalithic period into historical times.

The orthodox archaeological view of prehistoric religion paints a gory picture of bloodthirsty rites involving human sacrifices and cannibalism practised by barbaric tribes to propitiate the elemental forces of Nature which they feared. This lurid vision is not supported by the evidence of the ley-line system or by the astronomical observations made from the stone circles. It is true that the ancients practised so-called 'fertility rites' with a sexual content, both symbolic and literal, which would have shocked the seventeenth-century Puritans who destroyed many of the old stones and outlawed the erotic customs associated with them. However, it must be remembered that these rituals were carried out to improve the fertility of the land, crops, animals and humans. They were performed as a natural part of daily life without any feelings of guilt or the artificial aura of 'naughtiness' which surrounds sexuality today.

The evidence for human sacrifice at megalithic sites is circumstantial and depends on a modern interpretation based on prejudice about ancient cultures rather than on actual practice. While it is well known that human sacrifice played a role in ancient religious practices, it cannot be treated in isolation but must be viewed in perspective. Ancient humans had an approach to death totally different from the one found in modern society, where it remains the final taboo, at least in Western culture. The whole notion of human sacrifice is very difficult for a modern 'civilized' person to comprehend, as it is a concept we have never experienced in a religious context.

Sacrifice still exists, of course, as a powerful social element in our present-day culture. In our own century it is the young men who died in the trenches during the Great War or the millions who were gassed in the concentration camps who provide our cultural gesture towards human sacrifice on a mass scale.

While it is comforting to think that modern humans have progressed beyond an atavistic fear of winter nights when demons howl in the wind and ghosts lurk behind every tree, there is no evidence that the ancients who constructed the megalithic circles suffered this irrational fear of the dark. In fact, humankind's feelings in this direction appear to have developed only after we lost our intuitive awareness of the natural forces which surround us and were aided by religious images which conjured up imaginary powers of darkness to haunt our dreams. There is no logical reason, apart from our own projected fears, to believe that the astronomer priests worshipped at the megalithic sites because they feared the powers they invoked. On the contrary, this priesthood seems to have worked in harmony with the cosmic and elemental forces which they personified as the gods of Nature.

The religion of the megalith-builders was a very complex one. It involved a cult of the dead, with contact between the living and the spirits of the departed, the worship of the sun as a representation of the creative life force, the veneration of the moon and the Earth as symbols of the feminine principle and communication between humankind and the cosmic forces which they associated with certain stars and constellations. Viewed against this spiritual background, the astronomical observations at the stone circles are not merely an attempt by early humans to build primitive (or perhaps not so primitive!) computers which can record the passing of time. They in fact form the sacred foundation of a complicated and sophisticated view of the universe which is equal to any modern religious concept.

In prehistoric spirituality, the role of the feminine principle was very highly developed, and it is a theme which is frequently encountered in Earth Mysteries research. In the palaeolithic culture, the sacred nature of the feminine was an essential factor in both religious belief and practice. All over Europe figurines which are believed to represent the Goddess have been found dating from this period. These statues have been labelled 'Venus' figures by archaeologists and exhibit curiously uniform characteristics. In most cases the face is blank or featureless, the lower legs are narrow and taper to a point, but the breasts, thighs and buttocks are grotesquely exaggerated. The ancient artists who modelled these images deliberately emphasized the erogenous zones of the female body associated with sexuality and childbirth. There can be no doubt that the viewer is looking at a representation of the Great Mother Goddess whose attributes are fertility, sexuality and procreation.

One of the most striking of these 'Venus' figures was discovered at Laussel in France. It depicts a naked, faceless priestess or goddess holding in her right hand a ritual object which looks like a curved animal horn or which might be a representation of the lunar crescent. Inscribed on this object are thirteen lines which have been interpreted as the thirteen moons or months of the lunar year. The division of time by using the cycles of the moon was evidently known to the Old Stone Age people, passed down to the megalith-builders and then inherited by the Celtic Druids who used a lunar calendar.

The belief held by cultures all over the planet that in the distant past the gods came down from the sky and taught humanity the arts of civilization could also be connected with the astronomer priests. This belief is to be found in the Bible, where the Ben Elohim, the 'sons of God', see that 'the daughters of men' are fair and come down to Earth in human form to mate with them. When a race of giants is spawned from this illicit liaison and proceed the wreak magical havoc on ordinary humans, the Elohim causes a great flood to destroy the planet, saving only Noah and his ark laden with animals. Similar myths can be found in different cultures as far apart as Sumeria and South America.

In recent years the theory of the 'ancient astronauts' who visited the Earth in the ancient past and interfered with human evolution by genetic engineering has been the subject of many bestselling paperback books. The astronomical alignments of Stonehenge and other prehistoric monuments have led to speculation about these early contacts between extra-terrestrials and humanity. It has been suggested that the stone circles acted as UFO beacons and that ley lines were – and are – used as a kind of 'cosmic energy grid' to power alien spaceships.

Such theories have tended to remain at the fringe of Earth Mysteries research, and their propagation has led to ridicule from orthodox archaeologists who are opposed to the whole concept of ley lines. It should be remembered that this was the same archaeological establishment who refused to accept the evidence of astronomical observation from megalithic sites. Also the fact remains that the astronomer priests designed the stone circles to channel energies which we, with all modern scientific knowledge, still cannot fully understand or control.

The astronomical alignments of the megaliths which form the basis of the study of astro-archaeology provide us with the clues to the ancient wisdom possessed by the astronomer priests. The worship of the solar and lunar deities was used by prehistoric humans to personify the cosmic forces which they contacted at their sacred sites. They also used astronomical calculations to provide a ritual calendar which was used to celebrate a seasonal cycle of festivals involving the fertility of the land and the tribe. These religious practices formed the essence of a philosophical belief-system which included sacred measurement as a symbolic metaphor for understanding cosmic mysteries.

3

SPIRITUAL GEOMETRY

It becomes apparent that the various disciplines under the heading of Earth Mysteries have areas which overlap. This is because basically it is the study of a universal belief-system once practised all over the planet which has survived as isolated fragments concealed within ancient history, folklore, arcane knowledge and religious mythology. The obvious areas where similarities can be detected are pyramidology, ley lines, astro-archaeology and spiritual geometry.

The cosmological vision of the universe which is found in spiritual geometry presents the measurement of the physical world of form as a symbolic reflection of the spiritual realm from which, according to esoteric teaching, it manifested. Spiritual geometry proposes that once a state of perfect harmony existed in the universe, and it uses mathematical formulae as symbols to represent states of consciousness and stages on the path to spiritual perfection.

When humanity first began to erect structures to live in and as places of worship, standard forms of measurement were conceived to ensure they were in proportion. Several ancient civilizations, including those of the Greeks and the Egyptians, used such a standard unit of measurement. Similarities between ancient measurements can be discerned. For instance, twenty-four British miles are equal to twenty-five ancient Greek miles, while twenty-four Greek miles correspond to twenty-five Roman miles.

Numerical values were not only used in architecture but were also employed to define a universal cosmic pattern. This pattern could be found in music, astronomy, mathematics and art and were the subject of study by the pagan priesthoods. The Greeks believed in a homocentric system – one with man as the measure of all things. For this reason their measuring units were based on the dimensions of an average human body. This was not a unique concept, as many ancient measures used the distance between the wrist and the elbow of a human arm or the span of a hand as a reference.

The recognition of geometric patterns in Nature led to the establishment of a set of basic shapes which became the primary or foundation symbols of spiritual geometry as a mystical science. Possibly the earliest of these geometric forms was the circle. This can be found in the shape of stone circles and the early 'round houses' of prehistoric times. The circle was represented in the sky by both the lunar and solar discs which became the objects of veneration in ancient cultures as symbols of cosmic principles. It is a primary feminine symbol because of its roundness – representing the womb, and in primeval times both the sun and the moon were regarded by some cultures as feminine in gender. Additionally, the circle is a symbol of the wholeness and spiritual perfection which are the goal of the religious quest.

One of the other early recognizable geometric symbols was the square. This is symbolically the opposite of the circle in shape, and for this reason it came to represent the material world. Because it has four corners, it was regarded as a glyph of the compass points of north, south, east and west and their corresponding elemental forces of earth, fire, air and water. The square can be divided into four smaller squares, which, when their sides are removed, create the equal-armed cross of the elements. This cross was widely used in pagan cultures and pre-dates the unbalanced Calvary cross of Christianity by many thousands of years.

Two of the geometric symbols are historically linked – the pentagram and the hexagram. The former is in the shape of a five-pointed star and is often drawn in one interlocked movement; hence its popular name, the 'endless knot'. It was a symbol widely used by medieval magicians and was given several curious nicknames, including 'the wizard's foot' and 'the goblin cross'.

In Christian folklore the pentagram is reputed to represent the five wounds which Christ suffered during the crucifixion. However, in the occult tradition it is a symbol of the four elements plus the fifth element, ether or spirit. The alchemists believed the pentagram was a representation of a human being with the arms and legs outstretched. In this form it is a symbolic rendering of the hermetic axiom 'As above – so below'. This saying encapsulates the occult belief that man is a microcosm, a 'little world', of the macrocosm, the 'greater world', which is the universe. Reversed, with two points upwards, the pentagram traditionally symbolizes chaos, disharmony and the powers of darkness.

The hexagram is, as its name suggests, a six-pointed star composed of two interlaced triangles, one pointing upwards while the other points down. It represents duality, for its geometric form is a symbolic representation of the twin polarities which co-exist in the universe. These are light and darkness, good and evil, male and female, heat and cold, earth and air, water and fire etc. The dualistic nature of the hexagram features in alchemy, which, at an esoteric level, is concerned with the balancing of the male and female energies in the psyche and the integration of the opposites. The hexagram is the sacred symbol of the Jewish race and is sometimes called 'the Seal of Solomon'. This Hebrew king was widely credited with occult knowledge and magical powers and was responsible for the building of the temple in Jerusalem which was originally dedicated to Goddess-worship. The rituals of modern Freemasonry are derived from the murder of the architect of the temple who was slain by three of

his apprentices because he refused to reveal the secrets of his
sacred craft.

One of the most important, if sadly neglected, geometric
symbols is the *Vesica Piscis*. This is created by overlapping two
equal circles to form a composite figure. In pre-Christian times
it was a symbol of the Great Mother Goddess, representing the
source from which all life was born. The early Church adopted
this symbol because it appeared to be an abstract form of a fish,
which was used to represent the Christ as 'the fisher of men'.

The last of the primary geometric symbols is the triangle. Its
three points are mind, body and spirit, which are the three
components of the human entity. Upright, the triangle is the
phallic masculine principle, while reversed, with the apex
downwards, it is the feminine principle and a symbol of the
female sexual organs. In theosophical occultism the triangle is a
representation of the divine qualities of love, wisdom and
power; in Christianity it is the holy trinity of the Father, Son
and Holy Spirit; in Tantricism it is the god and goddess Shiva
and Shakti, while in alchemy it is the sacred essence of fire
(upright) and water (reversed) or matter and spirit.

In the pagan religions the universe and God were regarded as
indivisible. By measuring and quantifying the physical world, it
was believed that the secrets of divinity could be discovered.
Although a considerable amount of geometric knowledge was
formulated in the classical period, the megalithic people were
the first known exponents of geometric design and divine
measurement in respect to sacred architecture.

As we have seen, Alexander Thom had discovered that not
only were the megalithic circles based on a standard unit of
measurement but also utilized right-angled triangles in their
dimensions. Thom's surveys exposed the fact that many stone
circles used geometric patterns in their design. For instance,
the dimensions of the Moel ty Uchaf circle in Gwynedd, North
Wales, are centred on a pentagram; Borrowstone Ring circle in
the Lake District uses two seven-sided polygons, while Alan
Water circle in Scotland is based on an octagon.

The most famous circle in the British Isles, Stonehenge, has even been claimed by the Earth Mysteries writer John Michell as a geometric metaphor for the new city of Jerusalem in the apocryphal Gospel of St John in the New Testament. Michell regards St John as a sacred geomancer who was also a student of the Cabbala, the mystical teachings of Judaism. The Cabbalists were experts in spiritual geometry and the sacred meaning of numbers as the formula to unlock occult mysteries. According to esoteric tradition, the dimensions of the new Jerusalem outlined by St John were based on the symbol of a circle containing a square with another circle inside it. Michell claims that this symbol can be superimposed on the reconstructed plan of Stonehenge which was built to represent the 'sacred city' which has been one of the focuses of human myth for thousands of years.

Whether Stonehenge is truly a symbolic representation of the new Jerusalem or the 'sacred city' of pagan mythology is a matter for debate. However, several key numbers are found in the geometric construction of stone circles which relate to the religious beliefs of many different cultures and historical periods. These numbers include five and seven, which have a sacred significance in most spiritual traditions, and nine, which is associated with the moon in the pagan Old Religion. Five, as we know, is symbolic of the five elemental forces and also the five senses of the human body. The number seven was sacred to the shamans of Northern Europe, and the seven classical planets known to the Greeks, Romans and Chaldeans became the basis for the occult correspondences used in medieval magic.

The seven planets were linked with the seven days of the week, the seven colours of the spectrum and the seven notes of the classical musical scale. This septenary division of the planets, colours and days was originally derived from Babylonian sources, who used the seven-pointed star as the symbol of the goddess Ishtar, and formed the foundation of the ancient science of astrology. In Jewish mythology the Earth was created by Jehovah in seven days, and the number seven is mentioned in the Old Testament as a factor in the destiny of the children of Israel. It also can be found in the Revelation of St John which prophesies the end of the old order and the creation of a utopian society ruled by divine law and spiritual geometry.

The magico-spiritual influence of seven in Judaism may have been introduced as a result of the exposure of the Hebrew slaves held captive in Babylon to the religious beliefs of their masters. The biblical story of the building of the Tower of Babel may have been influenced by the sacred architecture of the Babylonians, especially the ziggurats (pyramid temples). These were erected in seven tiers, with each one representing one of the seven planets in Babylonian astronomy. The ziggurats were designed so they were orientated to the four points of the compass and were gateways between the material world and the realm of the gods. The apex of these pyramid-shaped temples was symbolic of the Pole Star, which the prehistoric shamans believed was the centre of the universe.

The legend of the Flood is another biblical myth which can be traced back to Babylonian or Sumerian mythology. Esoteric tradition teaches that Noah's ark was constructed using the principles of sacred geometry and measurements based, as in the Greek system, on the dimensions of the human body. Other accounts allege the ark was built using measurements which relate to the Earth's circumference, and this is particularly symbolic considering that its divine purpose was the preservation of the genetic seed of the planet.

Another Judaic sacred object which was allegedly the product of spiritual geometric principles was the Ark of the Covenant. Biblical scholars are still divided as to exactly what the Ark represents, and the description in Exodus 37:2-24, although detailed, poses more questions than it solves. The Ark is variously said to have contained the sacred scrolls of Jewish law, a record of sacred measurements or the stone tablets given to Moses by Jehovah.

The standard Hebrew measuring unit was a cubit, which was the average length of the human arm between the elbow and the end of the index finger. In normal circumstances a cubit was regarded as being about eighteen inches. The Ark of the Covenant was allegedly 2½ cubits (3¾ feet) in length by 1½ cubits (2¼ feet), which gives a parameter measurement of eight cubits (twelve feet). It has been speculated that, if the Ark was approximately one inch thick, its interior expressed in cubic inches would relate to the circumference of the Earth.

The Ark was contained within the Tabernacle, a travelling temple carried around by the Hebrews during their nomadic wanderings in the desert. In biblical lore the measurement of the Tabernacle was not produced by human hands but was dictated to the high priest by Jehovah. Its actual design was based on plans drawn up by two architects elected by the Israelites to perform this sacred task. The Tabernacle was always set up using a directional orientation facing east towards the rising sun. This deliberate procedure hints at an element of sun-worship. It is possible this orientation of the Tabernacle was connected with Egyptian temple-construction, as the Hebrews had been exposed to their religious ideas during the years of slavery before the exodus, and Moses is reputed to have been an initiate of the Egyptian mysteries.

The vestments worn by the Hebrew high priest were also highly symbolic and had links with spiritual geometry. He wore a square breastplate representing the physical world in which were embedded twelve semi-precious stones. Some occult authorities regard these stones as symbols of the twelve signs of the zodiac. The number twelve occurs quite often in Jewish religious belief, e.g. the twelve tribes of Israel, the twelve patriarchs of the Old Testament and the twelve apostles of the Christ.

In the classical period spiritual geometric theory was transformed by the works of Pythagoras, who gave his name to the right-angled triangle used by the megalith-builders. His life was shrouded in mystery, and the popular belief was that he was of divine birth and had incarnated in a human body to teach mortals. The accounts of his alleged miraculous birth resemble the later story of the Christ, for it is recorded that Pythagoras' father was told by the oracle at Delphi that his wife would bear a child who would be a benefactor to humanity and outshine all other men in beauty and wisdom. It was said that Pythagoras was the offspring of the solar god of healing, Apollo, and in later years his disciples even called him 'the Son of God'.

Although the circumstances of his birth are obscured by myth and legend, it is believed that Pythagoras was born around 600 BCE and was the son of a wealthy merchant. As a young man he took an interest in religious subjects and philosophy, was initiated into several esoteric fraternities and was conversant with the inner teachings of the Egyptian and Chaldean mysteries. He travelled to Egypt, Phoenicia and Asia and was taught by spiritual masters from all those lands.

When he returned from his wanderings, Pythagoras founded a university of spiritual philosophy at Crotona in southern Italy. There he gathered together a small group of disciples to whom he taught the arts of mathematics, music and astronomy. In common with most of the pagan mystery schools, the Pythagorean college admitted men and women on equal terms, and at the age of sixty Pythagoras married one of his young disciples and they had seven children.

Pythagoras' death, in common with his life, is surrounded by confusion and mystery. His outspoken views on contemporary religion and politics had won him few friends and made him generally unpopular. In one story an angry mob attacks the university, and Pythagoras is killed when it is razed to the ground. An alternative story has him murdered by renegade disciples who are incensed because he does not grant them the higher degrees of initiation. This sounds similar to the Masonic legend of Hiram Abiff, the architect of King Solomon's temple, who is ritually murdered by his apprentice masons.

Whatever the real truth about his violent death, at the hands of either the ignorant masses or those who resented his superior knowledge, the spiritual legacy bequeathed to humanity by Pythagoras was to be the foundation of the occult sciences in later European culture. Indirectly Pythagorean principles influenced such diverse areas of academic study as Gothic architecture, Renaissance art and even the quantum physics of the twentieth century. Pythagoras taught his disciples that God was *monad*, 'the one that is everything'. He described God as 'the Supreme Mind' which permeates the universe and is 'the primary cause of all things; the intelligence within all things and the power which controls all things'.

The central tenet of the Pythagorean philosophy is a model of the universe vibrating to the cosmic rhythm of celestial harmony. This universal harmony or inner perfection is the ethereal sinew which binds together the cosmos. Pythagoras argued that only by understanding geometry and the hidden meaning of numbers could man unlock the secrets of creation which existed within himself. It was this Pythagorean concept of universal harmony and perfection expressed through numerical values which degenerated in the Middle Ages into the divinatory art of numerology. This occult practice claimed to be able to describe a person's character and predict their destiny from an analysis of their name or birth date translated into numbers.

Pythagoras taught, passing on received knowledge from ancient sources, that everything in the universe has its own special numerical value and musical note which vibrates in accordance with its relationship to everything else in creation. In the Pythagorean cosmology, good and evil are not absolute extremes engaged in an eternal struggle for the mastery of the universe as they are represented in the dualistic religions such as Manicheanism and Judeo-Christianity. Pythagoras saw the powers of light and darkness as twin poles of a neutral power which is potentially both constructive and destructive. It is our individual reaction to the cosmic order, and whether we are in harmony or disharmony with the divine pattern, which produces the positive or negative states of existence morally categorized in our cultural terms of reference as 'good' and 'evil'.

Students of the Pythagorean college progressed through three degrees or stages of initiation which were the prototype of

later initiatory systems, including those of the medieval
Freemasons. The trinity was a powerful form to the
Pythagoreans and was symbolized as a triangle representing
the three-in-one, the synthesis of mind, body and spirit which
was the pre-requisite for spiritual enlightenment.

The teachings of Pythagoras divided the universe into three
realms: the Supreme World, the Superior World and the
Inferior World, which corresponded to the three degrees of
initiation. The first of these three worlds was the plane of
existence where life was created and from which flowed the
divine essence which permeated the universe. This world was
the realm of the Supreme Deity who was omnipotent,
omnipresent and omniscient and reconciled all opposites
within itself.

The second world was the realm of the immortals or the
mental plane of existence. Today we would regard this plane
as the home of the archetypes or primordial images described
in Jungian psychology as existing within the human psyche.
The immortals could be perceived by humankind only
through the reflections of their shadows cast on the material
world. The third world was the home of the mortal gods who
were the angels of biblical lore described in esoteric tradition
as the messengers of God who are evolved only a little more
than spiritually enlightened humans. This world is also the
elemental realm of the *devas*, the Nature spirits who are
responsible for the natural environment of the physical plane.

Pythagorean philosophy embraced the study of mathematics, geometry, music and astronomy as keys to
understanding the nature of God and the spiritual plane. It
regarded mathematics as the most important of the sciences,
for the numbers one to ten represented spiritual truths which
could be understood by the initiate who was versed in this
subject. A complete system of sacred geometry was based on
these numerical values and their primary significance in the
cosmic pattern.

Although Pythagoras was more spiritually aware than many
of his contemporaries, the practice of geometry in ancient

Greece took into account the theory of divine harmony expressed through sacred measurement and proportion. The Greek temples, such as the Parthenon in Athens, were designed to incorporate geometric theory which elevated architecture to an occult science. The Greeks were also instrumental in the revelation of the Golden Section, which later played a major role in Renaissance art. The Golden Section is the division of a line into two unequal parts, so that the lesser one is in the same proportion to the greater as the greater is to the whole. This proportion is to be found in Nature, including the human body, and forms the basis of ancient sacred measurements which relate architecture to the proportions inherent in the natural world.

With the coming of Christianity, the principles of spiritual geometry became less important in the construction of sacred buildings, at least on a conscious level. These principles were not completely lost, for many of the masons who erected the medieval Christian churches were secretly followers of the pagan Old Religion who had inherited the ancient wisdom. Many churches were erected on power centres which were previously places of pagan worship, and some of them contain extraordinary symbols in their architecture which are of pre-Christian origin. These include serpents and dragons, images of the Earth energy, the Green Man, who is the vegetation god of the pagan religion, and the Sheela-na-gig, with her legs open to expose her vagina, who is the Mother Goddess of the old fertility cults.

In the classical period the construction of the temples in Italy was supervised by the Roman College of Architects. When this college was disbanded at the beginning of the Christian era, its members fled to Comacina, an island on Lake Como, where they founded the Order of the Comacine Masters. This secret society was organized into lodges ruled by Grand Masters, and it had a tradition of passwords, secret codes and initiations. In the seventh century CE, when Italy was invaded by the Lombards, the order, who were trained in sacred geometry, were hired by the kings of Lombardy to build churches and cathedrals. The Order of the Comacini can be regarded as the forerunner of the masonic guilds who were formed to protect the rights of the builders of the medieval Gothic cathedrals.

The explosion of cathedral- and church-building which took place from the tenth century onwards can be connected to the rise of the monastic orders in Europe, the consolidation of the Roman Church's political power and the growth of the Marian cultus dedicated to the veneration of the Blessed Virgin Mary. Many of the early churches were patronized by the monastic orders or commissioned by wealthy rulers who wanted to raise grand monuments to the glory of God.

At least one of the monastic orders is said to have had knowledge of spiritual geometry and its use in the design of the Gothic cathedrals of medieval Europe. This fraternity was the Order of the Poor Knights of the Temple of Solomon in Jerusalem, more popularly known as the Knights Templar. The order was founded in the twelfth century by three Frankish knights as a band of warrior monks who had the responsibility of protecting the pilgrim routes to the Holy Land. Both the Templars and the medieval masonic guilds regarded the temple of King Solomon in Jerusalem as a holy site. It has been suggested that the Templars were inheritors of a secret geomantic tradition which was passed on to the Freemasons when the order was suppressed by the Pope in 1314.

The Templars had sworn vows of poverty and chastity drawn up by St Bernard, who was a devotee of the Marian cultus, but during their 200-year history the order achieved considerable political power and acquired vast amounts of material wealth. Templar castles formed a network covering Europe, the Mediterranean and the Middle East; they had established an international trading system and were recognized as the papal bankers. Their eventual downfall was the result of a plot by the Vatican and the French Court, who considered the order had become too powerful and was threatening their joint interests. Criminal charges were made against the Templars, including the practice of heresy, blasphemy, treason and unnatural sexual activities. It was said that during their occupation of the Holy Land the knights had made secret pacts with the Saracens, become addicted to Arabian occult practices and even been converted to Islam.

As well as protecting the pilgrims who travelled to the sacred sites of Christianity in the Middle East, the Templars were dedicated to the defence of Solomon's Temple in Jerusalem, and their headquarters was set up on its site. It was rumoured that the Templars planned to restore the temple to its former glory before it was destroyed, but this idea had to be abandoned when the Saracens recaptured Jerusalem. It has been suggested by some biblical scholars that the original temple was a shrine to the pagan goddess Astarte, who was worshipped in Canaan before the arrival of the Israelites. It is said that Solomon imported architects and masons from Tyre in Lebanon to design and build his temple. Tyre was one of the ancient centres for Goddess-worship in the Middle East and was a Templar stronghold in the thirteenth century.

The Templars built their own churches all over Europe but especially in England, Germany, France and Holland. The majority of these churches were round or octagonal in shape. As we noted earlier, churches with circular graveyards are a sign that medieval religious sites were once pagan temples. The design of the Templar round churches was based on the druidic sacred groves, the megalithic circles and the circular temples of classical Greece and Rome. By building their churches in this unusual shape, the Templars were expressing the fact that their inner beliefs were derived from paganism and not Christianity.

While the early Christian churches were built on pagan sites, it seems unlikely that the priests who followed this policy were consciously aware of the Earth energy which could be found at these ancient power centres. The medieval masonic guilds, which later developed into the lodges of speculative Freemasonry, were more aware of the spiritual aspects of the siting and construction of sacred buildings. This knowledge may have been shared by a minority of the European rulers and high-ranking clerics who commissioned the medieval cathedral-building.

One example of this occult or hidden knowledge can be found in the architecture of Chartres Cathedral in France, which brings together the pagan religion, Templar wisdom, masonic expertise and geometric design in the classic tradition of Gothic architecture. Early Christian pilgrims visited Chartres because it was a shrine to the Black Virgin. Her image was located in an underground grotto beneath the church which was also the site of a holy well. The statue of the Virgin had been carved from the hollowed-out trunk of an ancient pear tree and was blackened with age; hence its title. It was venerated in the Middle Ages as a representation of the Virgin Mary depicted in a seated position with the infant Jesus cradled on her knee.

Chartres seems to be a Christian shrine but local legend claims that the Black Virgin had been placed in the grotto in pagan times by the Druids. It was said the archdruid had a dream in which an angelic being announced that a new god had been born of a virgin. The Druids carved the statue of the Black Virgin and placed it in the cave shrine. The early Christians who visited Chartres were amazed to find the local pagans worshipping a virgin and child, and the shrine became a place of pilgrimage.

The mound where the Christian shrine to the Black Virgin was erected was also the site of a dolmen (burial chamber) dating from the prehistoric period. The story of the archdruid's dream may be based on fact, as Chartres was a pre-Christian centre for the worship of the Mother Goddess. The area around the cathedral has many ancient monuments, including the remains of stone circles, standing stones and burial mounds. In the Iron Age Chartres was especially sacred to the Celts, who called it 'the sanctuary of sanctuaries'. The mound on which the medieval cathedral stands was said to have been the site of a druidic college which drew its psychic energy from the shrine of the Black Virgin/Mother Goddess in the cave below it.

In the Dark Ages Chartres became a focus for Christian

pilgrimage with the conversion of the local pagans to the new religion. However, it was not until the twelfth century that the present cathedral was built. It replaced a church attached to a Benedictine monastery and hospital which was destroyed by fire in 1194. The mystery of how a small town like Chartres financed the construction of the cathedral has puzzled historians, and there are hints that the heretical Order of the Knights Templar were involved. It is also known that the Benedictines were very wealthy, and it is possible that the superiors of the order made funds available, but why they should choose such a blatantly pagan site is curious.

An examination of the architecture of Chartres Cathedral makes it clear that it has many interesting geometric features. Unlike most churches of the Middle Ages, the cathedral is aligned not to the east but to the north-east. It has been suggested that this change of axis is so that the building can take advantage of the Earth energy which flows through the ancient mound, rather than any Christian observance. In addition the proportions of the cathedral are based on the Golden Number, the perfect unit of measurement which embodies divine harmony in numerical form. The plan of the cathedral's apse is based on the seven-pointed star which, as we have seen earlier, originated in pagan symbolism.

Chartres has several other unusual features which make it an intriguing religious site from both an orthodox and a heterodox viewpoint. In the nave is carved a labyrinth whose design dates back to megalithic times. In ancient religious ceremonies the labyrinth was used for initiation rites. The initiates 'walked' the maze or labyrinth until they reached the centre. In Christian lore pilgrims crawled on their knees around the maze in a symbolic re-enactment of the journey by the Christ to his great initiation on the cross.

The rose window at Chartres brings into play the correspondence between light and architecture that has been a keynote of sacred architecture for thousands of years. Most of the Gothic cathedrals had stained glass windows decorated with scenes from the Old and New Testaments. The traditional view is that these windows were placed in medieval churches for their aesthetic value as works of sacred art. Louis Charpentier, a French historian and writer on esotericism who has studied Chartres, has a different opinion. He believes that the art of stained glass making was an occult practice. Charpentier claims that when the light is filtered through this type of window its nature is subtly changed, as if by an alchemical process. This transformation can produce spiritual vibrations or a psychic atmosphere which is experienced by anyone standing in the sacred building, and it can alter their state of normal consciousness.

This seems to be a far-fetched idea until you consider that modern scientific research has proved that different colours of the spectrum can have tangible effects, both psychologically and physically, on the human organism. There is no reason to think that such effects could not have been duplicated by the medieval masons. It is known from the esoteric practice of colour healing that the light spectrum can create beneficial results in terms of health and psychological moods. It is inconceivable that this fact was not known to practitioners of the occult tradition in the Middle Ages, for the use of colour to heal dates back to the pre-Christian era.

Chartres, like the megalithic burial chambers and the Egyptian pyramids, utilizes light in another way. Every year at midday on 21 June, the date of the summer solstice, a shaft of light passes through a stained glass window on the western side of the transept of the cathedral and strikes a small metal inset on a flagstone in the nave.

Charpentier believes that the Knights Templar were involved in the construction of Chartres Cathedral and may have financed the building work in order to leave a monument which displayed the occult symbols of their heretical religious tradition. He points out that the cathedral contains a statue of Melchisedek, the ancient Hebrew priest king who was the guardian of the Holy Grail. In the Middle Ages it was popularly believed that the Templars were the guardians of this sacred receptacle which in Christian mythology was the cup used by the Christ at the Last Supper and in pagan myth was the cauldron of divine inspiration owned by the Great Goddess. An image of the Ark of the Covenant, which Charpentier alleges contained tables of the sacred measurements used in spiritual geometry, can also be found in a prominent position in the cathedral. Finally, Chartres was originally a shrine to the Black Virgin, who was a prime object of veneration by the Templars and their sister fraternity the Priory of Sion.

From the evidence, the conclusion has to be reached that Chartres Cathedral is a Christian edifice built on a pagan power centre by a brotherhood of masons who were aware of its spiritual significance as an ancient sacred site. Whoever was responsible for commissioning the building, whether Christian monks or heretical knights, knew this and deliberately introduced into its architecture geomantic and geometric features which seven centuries later can be decoded to prove that the building is a monument to a religious tradition older than Christianity.

Another sacred place which is of significance to both Christians and pagans is Glastonbury in Somerset, which provides a meeting-place for both religions. In pre-Christian times the conical hill outside the medieval market town, known as the Tor, was regarded by the Celts as hollow and the entrance to the Otherworld. In an even earlier age a stone circle is said to have stood on the Tor where there now rests the ruins of a chapel dedicated to the guardian of the gates of Hell, St Michael.

Around the Tor the base of the hill is encircled by a maze, in the surrounding countryside is mapped out a terrestrial zodiac, and below the Tor is the Chalice Garden, where a holy well dedicated to the Goddess is situated. The maze, the well and the zodiac will be examined in later chapters; the subject here is the geometric significance of Glastonbury as revealed in its Christian remains and pagan origins. Today the Glastonbury area is regarded as a prime site for investigation by Earth Mysteries students and in recent years has also become the centre for a flourishing New Age counter-culture.

In local legend, Glastonbury was the place where the first

Christian church was founded in Britain. After the crucifixion, the uncle of Jesus, called Joseph of Arimathea, travelled to the West Country with a group of twelve disciples. Within sight of the Tor on Wearyall Hill, it is said Joseph thrust his staff into the earth. It immediately took root and blossomed into a flowering thorn. According to popular folklore, this miraculous tree flowered only to coincide with Christmas, or the winter solstice, and Easter, or the vernal equinox. An offshoot of the original thorn can still be seen in the grounds of the ruined medieval abbey, and it still flowers every year.

Joseph obtained permission from the local Druids to purchase a piece of land below the Tor which consisted of twelve hides (1,440 acres). On this was built a wood-and-wattle chapel which was dedicated to the Virgin Mary. Several of the Druids were allegedly converted to the new faith, for they found it easier to worship the Virgin, whom they regarded as another version of the Celtic Mother Goddess, and a Christian community was established in the shadow of the pagan Tor.

Why did Joseph settle at Glastonbury? Esoteric tradition says he was no stranger to the area and was well aware of its importance as a sacred power centre. As a wealthy merchant he had paid regular visits to the West Country to trade for tin from the Cornish mines. On one of these trips, it is claimed, Joseph brought his nephew Jesus, who was initiated into a local druidic college. This legend formed the inspiration behind the epic poem 'Jerusalem' by the eighteenth-century visionary William Blake which pinpoints Albion (Britain) as the site for the new city of Jerusalem described in the mystical Revelation of St John.

The original church built by Joseph and his followers was preserved by the monks of the medieval abbey, who coated it with lead. In 1184, ten years before the destruction of the original church at Chartres, the chapel at Glastonbury was burned down. The medieval monks built a stone chapel on the site using the same geometric proportions as the original and dedicated it to both Joseph, who had been canonized by then, and the Virgin Mary. This building still stands within the precincts of the abbey.

In the Middle Ages the abbey at Glastonbury was one of the wealthiest religious houses in the country. The Domesday Book records the fact that the twelve hides were exempt from tax. Even the king had no power over the abbey, and its abbot was represented in ecclesiastical councils as the senior member of the British Church. This was because Glastonbury was the original foundation of Christianity in the islands.

This privileged situation came to a sudden and violent end with the onset of the English Reformation in the sixteenth century which destroyed the political power of the Roman Church. When Henry VIII closed down the monasteries, the king's commissioners accused the monks at Glastonbury of concealing the treasure belonging to the abbey. The last abbot, Richard Whiting, was hanged on the Tor, and the abbey buildings were levelled, leaving only the ruins which are visible today. Speculation was rife over the nature of the treasure allegedly hidden by the monks, especially as the abbot was willing to die without revealing its location. Rumours abounded of underground tunnels and secret hiding-places under the abbey, and of a cave inside the Tor which had been used for initiations by the Druids. It was even claimed that Joseph of Arimathea had buried the cup used at the Last Supper in Glastonbury.

The abbey is still in ruins today, despite many attempts over the centuries to restore it for Roman worship. In the 1900s these plans were rendered impossible when the Anglican Church obtained control over the ruins, which had been purchased by the nation.

In 1907 the Diocesan Trust which administered the abbey ruins appointed an architect, Frederick Bligh Bond, to carry out archaeological excavations on the site. This appointment became a matter of great controversy, for Bligh Bond was fascinated by psychic matters. During the excavations he used automatic writing to communicate with a dead monk called Johannes de Glaston (John of Glastonbury), who had been at the abbey in the fifteenth century. This discarnate entity provided Bligh Bond with detailed information on the layout and construction of the abbey in medieval times.

As a result of this mediumistic contact, the architect was able to locate the lost chapel in the abbey, working on information provided by the deceased monk. Unfortunately Bligh Bond's clerical employers were less than delighted at these unexpected results and the unorthodox method used to obtain them. When Bligh Bond published a book about his psychic experiences in 1918, they were forced to sack him as Director of Archaeological Excavations at the abbey.

Bligh Bond's spirit guide provided some interesting details of the spiritual geometry of the abbey. In one communication he even refers to a brother monk who was the official geomancer to the abbey. In common with many other medieval churches, Glastonbury had been designed using sacred measurements and divine proportion. Bligh Bond discovered that the architecture of the abbey was centred on a grid consisting of thirty-six squares, each measuring seventy-four feet. He also found out that the chapel of St Joseph and St Mary was built using geometric dimensions relating to the area of land occupied by the original Christian settlement in the first century CE.

Led on by clues provided by Johannes, Bligh Bond realized that the chapel plan was based on a circle enclosing a pentagon and a *vesica piscis*. Translated from the Latin, this means 'fish bladder' and was a reference to the use of this ancient symbol by the early Church as a glyph for the Christ, who was the avatar of the Age of Pisces, the zodiac sign of the Fishes. In the esoteric tradition, this symbol is a sign of the fusion of matter and spirit and a representation of the female vagina, which was a venerated object in Goddess-worship. In the twelfth century the historian William of Malmesbury describes patterns of stones inlaid in triangles and squares on the chapel floor which conceal a 'sacred enigma'. Johannes claimed that the abbey was 'a message in stone' and that the keys to it could be seen in the designs on the chapel floor which had been destroyed. He says, 'In ye floor of ye Mary's Chappel was ye Zodiac, that all might see and understand the mystery.'

Bligh Bond stated that the early Christian settlement founded by St Joseph at Glastonbury was also laid out by geometric principles. The twelve hides of land purchased from the Druids were symbolic of the twelve signs of constellations of the zodiac. This settlement, as outlined by Bligh Bond, consisted of a round church dedicated to the Virgin which was encircled by twelve cells used by the disciples. These in turn were surrounded by a circular wall or earthwork. The Earth Mysteries writer John Michell has claimed that this plan was another example of the layout of the 'sacred city' of Jerusalem described by St John in the Book of Revelations. He compares it with the allegorical city of Plato's *Republic*, which has been claimed to be the lost continent of Atlantis, and the groundplan of Stonehenge.

Glastonbury has been recognized as an ancient site of Goddess-worship, and there are strong indications that this cult survived into the Christian era in the area. The dedication of the abbey chapel to the Blessed Virgin Mary is one obvious sign. Bligh Bond also made another interesting archaeological find inside the abbey grounds which may be linked with the pagan worship of the feminine principle: he unearthed an egg-shaped stone measuring approximately three feet by two feet which had a cavity hollowed out of its centre.

Bligh Bond considered this find as evidence that the site of the abbey had been a pagan temple in the distant past. In ancient times these egg-shaped stones were called *omphalos*, meaning 'the centre of the world' or 'the source of inspiration'. An *omphalos* was discovered at the temple in Delphi, which was a famous oracle of the Goddess attended by her priestesses, known as sibyls, who uttered prophecies. Although often mistaken as a phallic symbol, the *omphalos* was in fact a sign of Goddess-worship and a representation of the cervix.

One odd numerical fact at Glastonbury is that, according to Bligh Bond's calculations, the length of the abbey was

originally 666 feet. This number is regarded by evangelical
Christians as the special sign of the Great Beast in Revelations
who is the Anti-Christ. John Michell, however, has claimed
that the proportions of the abbey are based on the megalithic
yard used to design the stone circles. He says 666 is a solar
number which has nothing to do with Satan or the Anti-Christ
but was associated with the pagan sun gods.

Glastonbury and Chartres are examples of ancient sacred
sites and power centres which have been sanctified over the
centuries by both pagan and (heretical) Christian worship.
They offer evidence of the continued tradition of spiritual
geometry surviving into the Middle Ages through the
activities of the masonic brotherhood of cathedral-builders
who were also occult initiates.

With the end of the magnificent period of Gothic cathedral
construction, the science of sacred geometry and the art of the
geomancer gradually faded into superstitious obscurity. The
old masonic guilds were transformed into the speculative
lodges of Freemasonry. Their members translated the
practical geometry of the operative masons into esoteric
symbolism which was used as a blueprint for spiritual
perfection.

With the Renaissance, many of the lost aspects of classical
paganism were revived specifically as an inspiration for the
artists of the period. However, this revival also included an
interest in the sacred architecture of classical history,
including the pagan temples of Greece and Rome. During the
period from the end of the fifteenth century to the middle of
the sixteenth, many round churches were built. This
shortlived attempt to revive the principles of sacred geometry
was condemned by clerical reactionaries, who saw it as a
resurgence of paganism in a Christian guise. It was declared
that the circular shape of the new churches should be
abandoned in favour of the cross-shaped design which takes its
form from the symbol of the crucified Christ.

This development did not, however, spell the end of the use
of geometric principles in sacred architecture. In the 1600s Sir

Christopher Wren, who was an initiate of the Fraternity of the
Rosy Cross, or Rosicrucians, rebuilt the Gothic cathedral of St
Paul's in the City of London using traditional geometric
symbolism. The inner enclosure of the cathedral has
proportions identical to those of the Great Pyramid, the
Hebrew Tabernacle and the temple of Solomon. As an occult
initiate, Wren was well aware of the esoteric symbolism of
designing the cathedral, so that its overall height is 365 feet,
representing the number of days in a year.

The sacred science of spiritual geometry is an attempt by
human builders to recreate a system of divine harmony on the
Earth. The great Gothic cathedrals, such as Nôtre Dame in
Paris, which has been described as an allegorical symbol of
hermetic occultism carved in stone, were designed by the
medieval masons as replacements for the pagan temples built
in accordance with sacred measurements. Spiritual geometry
is a symbolic blueprint of creation which has been understood
by initiates of the ancient wisdom since the dawn of history.

4

HILL FIGURES

Among the most fascinating enigmas of Earth Mysteries research are the gigantic hill figures carved across the British landscape, especially in southern England. The majority of these carvings date from early times but some new ones have been added in recent history, and they include crosses and regimental badges. Although these later additions are interesting from a socio-psychological angle, they are of little interest to Earth Mysteries researchers. Their attention is drawn instead to the thirty or so major hill figures in the English countryside which are of pagan origin.

These images can be classified into main groupings – white horses and giants. The term 'hill figures' to describe them was invented by the late Sir Flinders Petrie, who was an archaeologist specializing in Ancient Egyptian remains. Petrie believed that the hill figures were not of Saxon, Celtic or Romano-British origin but dated back to the Bronze Age. The difficulty with trying to establish any firm date for these figures is one that has caused many problems over the years. Any attempt to date them accurately has to rely largely on inspired guesswork, their physical appearance or snippets of local folk-tradition about their legendary origins or historical use.

The largest concentration of hill figures belongs to the White Horse category. These can be found mainly in a relatively small area of central southern England covering Wiltshire, Warwickshire and Berkshire. Why these images should appear in only one particular region is a mystery. It has been suggested that all the White Horses are of Iron Age origin and date from the time when southern England was inhabited by Celtic tribes who worshipped the horse goddess Epona.

The sacred horse played an important role in ancient religious beliefs which survived in historical times as folk-customs. Today the hobby-horse is merely seen as a child's toy but in the past it was the object of folk-rituals which were a debased memory of pre-Christian horse-worship. In the Middle Ages the hobby-horse was a leading character in the May Day revels, which were relics of pagan rites to welcome back the sun from its winter hibernation. The May Day hobby was usually a wooden horse head attached to a pole. It was held by one of the dancers, who pranced along holding it between his legs. A variation on this design was the Hooden Horse, a horse mask with a mane attached to a hoop which was draped with cloth to represent the animal's body. The Hooden Horse was often decorated with ribbons, multi-coloured threads and bells. A dancer hid under the 'skirt' of the horse and operated its movements like a giant puppet.

In some instances the mask of the figure was an actual horse's skull, and one example of this is the Welsh *Mari Lwyd*. This old custom has been described as a Celtic horse ceremony, and its practice survived in parts of Glamorgan and Carmenthenshire into the 1950s. The *Mari Lwyd* ('grey mare') made its debut at New Year or Twelfth Night. It consisted of a horse's skull with a string attached to the jaw so its operator could snap it open or shut. The skull was fixed to the top of a five-foot pole, and a white sheet was draped over it. Coloured ribbons were used to adorn the skull, which had pieces of bottle glass for eyes, ears made of cloth, and reins sewn with tiny bells.

The *Mari Lwyd* visited houses in the district accompanied by a motley crew of characters from folklore, including Punch and

Judy, the Merryman and the Leader, who all wore bizarre costumes decorated with bells and ribbons and played musical instruments. Traditional songs or wassails were sung outside the house, and if the correct ritual responses were received from inside, the *Mari Lwyd* entered. After chasing and kissing all the women of the household, the horse and its party were treated to mulled wine and mince-pies.

This ritual has been identified by folklorists as the folk-survival of a pagan winter solstice rite in honour of the Celtic horse goddess Epona previously worshipped in South Wales. Epona was depicted in ancient art as a naked woman riding on a white horse or a goose. She has been variously identified with the nursery-rhyme character Mother Goose, the lady who rode a white horse to Banbury Cross and the pagan original of Coventry's Lady Godiva. The Celts regarded her as a Great Mother figure but she is also associated with fertility, sexuality and the underworld.

Elements of pagan horse-worship could still be found in the medieval period. In Ireland the king was crowned in a ceremony which had echoes of the Celtic reverence for the goddess of horses. The Welsh historian Giraldus Cambrensis recorded an account of this ritual when he travelled through Ulster between 1183 and 1185. He described how a white mare was presented to the king who 'embraced it as he would a woman'. The horse was then sacrificed, cut into pieces and boiled in a cauldron. The king sat in this container, the resulting broth was poured over him and he drank from it. This barbaric practice has been compared with Hindu rituals of horse sacrifice, and it is to be noted that the Celts and the Hindus shared a common Aryan ancestry.

Two of the most famous relics of Celtic horse-worship in England are to be found in the hobby-horses of Padstow in Cornwall and Minehead in Somerset.

At Padstow the hobby is known affectionately as Old Hoss, and the present incumbent of the role dates from the nineteenth century. It has a small head with grey whiskers, a lolling red tongue and white-circled eyes. A tall, pointed cap covers the operator's head, and below the face mask is a wooden hoop from which a black drape falls to the ground, concealing his body.

The hobby-horse procession begins its first circuit of the Cornish village at midnight on 30 April, May Eve, the day before the old Celtic festival of Beltane. The dancers sing what is known as the Night Song under the windows of the houses belonging to prominent town people or welcomed villages. At dawn the Old Hoss does his rounds again, but this time the troupe of dancers sing the Day Song which welcomes the arrival of the summer. The hobby-horse chases the young women of the village, and it is considered lucky if he catches you. Locals say that any girl who is caught by Old Hoss will marry before the summer is out.

This fertility aspect of the traditional hobby-horse features in most of the folk-rituals associated with it. In the sixteenth century, when the term 'hobby-horse' was first used, it was also a slang word for a 'loose person' or a prostitute of either sex. This erotic connotation links the hobby-horse with both the May Day frolics, which were banned by the Puritans because of their blatant sexual content, and the pagan fertility rites of the horse goddess.

The Minehead hobby-horse seems to be a racial memory of pre-Christian sea-worship. It is popularly known as 'the Sailor's Horse' and is under the guardianship of the current owners of the quay. In common with its Cornish cousin, Minehead's hobby has a conical cap, but its face mask has humanoid rather than equine features. Its 'skirt' is painted with circles and is covered with ribbons and patches of silk and velvet.

As in the Cornwall custom, the Minehead horse acts as the harbinger of summer. In the nineteenth century it used to set out on the evening of 30 April and went to the local crossroads. There a drum was played and villagers danced around it. At dawn on May Day the hobby-horse ventured forth again, accompanied by the prettiest girl in the village, who was elected as the May Queen for the day. Tradition has

Coldrum stones

Callanish standing stones, Isle of Lewis

Men-an-Tol, near Madron, Cornwall

The Womb of Ceridwen, Pentre Ifan, West Wales

Avebury

Stonehenge

Silbury Hill

Glastonbury Tor

The Great Pyramid at Giza

The White Horse of Uffington, Wiltshire

Entrance to burial chamber, Wayland's Smithy, Oxfordshire

The Cerne Abbas Giant, Dorset

The Long Man of Wilmington, East Sussex

Chanctonbury Ring, West Sussex

it there once was a May King and that both rode on the horse's back.

This archaic custom has many pagan elements. May Day, as we have seen, was an old Celtic festival to greet the arrival of the summer. In ancient times crossroads were sacred ground dedicated to the Goddess in her aspect as ruler of the underworld. The gathering of the hobby-horse and its human attendants at this place on the night before Beltane is a symbolic act of death before the rebirthing ceremony of the next day. The crowning of the May King and Queen may seem like a quaint folk-custom but in fact it is a sanitized relic of the ritual mating of the human representatives of the Green Man and the Earth Mother at the springtime fertility rites.

Pagan horse-worship survived not only in this type of folk-tradition but also in the secret society of the Horseman's Word or the Horse Whisperers which met in rural areas, especially East Anglia and Scotland. Membership of this cult was restricted to blacksmiths, farriers, stable lads, farmers and anyone else who worked with horses. The Horsemen were said to possess a magical secret which was capable of calming and controlling the wildest horse.

Blacksmiths in general were traditionally regarded as powerful magicians because they controlled both fire and horses in their work. Their belief dates back to a time when horses were first introduced into Europe, when anyone who worked with them gained a magical aura. A new horseshoe from a smithy was valued as a potent charm to ward off evil forces. Nailed over a barn or cottage door, with the horns upright so the luck would not run out, it was seen by country people as the symbol of the pagan moon goddess. The nails used by the blacksmith to fix the horseshoe were also used in folk magic and were prized by witches for their spells.

Initiation into the Society of Horsemen was a terrifying ordeal. It traditionally took place on Hallowe'en, 31 October, which was the eve of the Celtic festival of Samhain which marked the end of summer and the beginning of winter. Members of the cult were called to the meeting, usually in a

remote barn, by the leader, who sent them a horse's hair as a
sign. Every member was expected to bring a loaf of bread, a
jar of berries and a bottle of whisky to be shared afterwards as
a ritual meal.

The neophyte was led blindfolded to the rendezvous by a
senior Horseman, who knocked three times and whinnied to
gain admittance. The would-be member knelt with his left
foot bare and his left hand raised. He then recited extracts
from the Bible backwards. When this was over, he was
instructed to shake hands with Old Nick, and the cloven hoof
of a goat or a ram was thrust into his hand. Having survived
this ordeal without showing any signs of fear, the new initiate
had his blindfold removed, was introduced to his fellow
Horsemen and was entrusted with the secret words used to
charm wild horses.

The pagan background of horse-worship and its survival
into historical times will be seen to be significant when we
examine perhaps the most famous of the many equine hill
figures, the White Horse of Uffington. This image has become
shrouded in mystery, myth and legend which have obscured
its real significance. It is situated about two miles south of the
village of Uffington in Berkshire and is about a quarter of a
mile north-east of the Iron Age hill-fort of Uffington Castle.
The White Horse is carved on a north escarpment of the
Berkshire Downs some 500 feet above the Vale of the White
Horse. Interestingly the White Horse can only be properly
viewed from a distance or from the air, which has predictably
led to speculation about UFOs and ancient astronauts. On a
clear day it can be seen from Swindon in Wiltshire to the west
of the Vale and from Abingdon in Oxfordshire in the east. It is
claimed that with the right atmospheric conditions the hill
figure can be seen over twenty miles away.

The White Horse is situated on the prehistoric trackway
known as The Ridgeway, dating from the neolithic period.
Above the hill figure this old green road converges with the
Icknield Way, which was used by the Romans. About a mile
from the White Horse is a burial mound known as Wayland's

Smithy. In Norse myth Wayland was the blacksmith of the gods who forged their weaponry. There is a local tradition that any traveller who left his horse at the Smithy on the night of the full moon could return at dawn and find it shod with silver horseshoes. This suggests the ancient worship of the moon and horses at the site.

Below the White Horse is an artificial-looking mound known as Dragon Hill. This is reputed to be one of the sites where St George killed the dragon. When Christianity replaced the old pagan ways, the Earth energy was regarded as an evil force and was symbolically represented as a serpent or dragon slain by shining knights on white horses. Dragon Hill is also said to be the place where UFOs touch down, according to those who believe the White Horse has extra-terrestrial connections.

The area around the hill figure must have been of some importance to the megalithic culture. As well as Wayland's Smithy there is evidence of a number of rows of standing stones which once stood in front of Ashdown House, a few miles from the White Horse. These stone rows covered an area of 266 yards by 533 yards, and some of the individual stones were ten feet high. Unfortunately no trace can be found of this outstanding megalithic monument today, and it is presumed that the standing stones were broken up and used in local building-projects.

The White Horse of Uffington is believed to be the oldest of all the hill figures in existence. Its unusual shape has led to some speculation that it is not, in fact, a horse at all but is supposed to be the legendary dragon killed by St George. However, the stylized shape of the horse is a typical Celtic design and can be found on coins minted for Boadicea in the 1st century CE. This ancient Celtic queen led the Icenia tribe who worshipped the horse goddess Epona. The Uffington horse has been compared with stylized examples of Celtic steeds found on buckets unearthed at Aylesford in Kent and at Marlborough on the Wiltshire downs. Archaeologists have tentatively dated the Uffington hill figure to the late Iron Age, c. first century BCE, but it may even be of Bronze Age origin.

Rock carvings in Sweden from that period depict horses which are almost identical to the one at Uffington.

In length, from the end of its nose to the tip of its tail, the White Horse is approximately 365 feet, the number of days in a solar year. Its greatest width is ten feet, which is at the middle section of its stomach. It has a beak-like snout and one large eye made up of two circles carved in the chalk.

The first written reference to the Uffington hill figure was made during the reign of Henry II (1154–89), when the name 'White Horse Hill' was used to describe its locality. A manuscript in Corpus Christi College, Cambridge, from the fourteenth century mentions the White Horse as one of the wonders of Britain and second only to Stonehenge. The seventeenth-century antiquarian John Aubrey regarded the Uffington horse as the standard of the Saxon warlord Hengist, who founded the county of Kent in the fifth century CE.

In 1738 the Rev. Francis Wise, a fellow of Trinity College and the keeper of the Radcliffe Library, penned the first written description of the White Horse. Wise credited King Alfred with its carving and caused a controversy by deleting its distinctive Celtic characteristics when he reproduced a drawing of the hill figure. His misrepresentation of the image as a natural-looking horse was corrected in 1813, when Lyson produced a more accurate illustration in his *Britannica*.

The Uffington horse was the centre of a local folk-custom known as 'scouring', which may have been a throwback to paganism. This event took place approximately every seven years and was accompanied by heavy drinking, feasting and general merrymaking. The seven-year cycle is interesting, considering the sacredness of this number in ancient times. When Wise wrote about the 'hill scouring' in the eighteenth century, it was even then an old-established practice which had been carried out for generations.

A graphic description of this folk ritual was given in Thomas Hughes' Victorian novel *The Scouring of the White Horse*, published in 1857. The scouring was an excuse for a two-day fair, horse-racing, a circus, competition and rural games which included rolling wheels down the hillside. The winner was awarded a local cheese. The actual scouring, or cleaning of the weeds and grass from the chalk outline of the hill figure, was performed by a special gang of workmen who were provided with cakes and ale by the lord of the manor. It was reported that when the scouring was held on Whit Monday in 1780 an amazing 30,000 people from all the country turned up to witness it.

The last recorded organized scouring of the White Horse took place in the 1850s, and by 1880 it was so overgrown that few of its features could be discerned. In 1884, however, it was recut and in 1892 Lady Craven paid for it to be scoured. By the turn of the century the White Horse had returned to its neglected state but today it is well preserved, due to the efforts of the National Trust, who in 1979 took over its welfare from the government.

Uffington can safely be regarded as an important centre of the pagan Old Religion in ancient times. Its nearness to Wayland's Smithy, with its folk-tales of moon-, horse- and fire-worship; the legend of St George killing the dragon on the mound, which also features in the Padstow hobby-horse ceremony, and the White Horse itself, symbolizing the Celtic goddess Epona, are all evidence of this fact.

Another interesting hill figure which is connected with pagan horse-worship is the White Horse at Westbury, Wiltshire, only a few miles from Uffington across country. It is located on a slope of the Bratton Downs about two miles from the village of Westbury and a mile south-west of the hamlet of Bratton. The horse faces west and has been carved below the Iron Age hill-fort of Bratton Camp which has a neolithic burial mound within its earthworks. The hill figure is approximately 180 feet long, with a width of 108 feet.

The present form of the hill figure dates only from the eighteenth century but was apparently carved over the original beast, which was far older. This first horse may have been of Saxon origin, as stories link it with the exploits of King Alfred in this part of the country. It has also been linked with the name of King Arthur, which could mean a Celtic origin.

Illustrations of the earlier White Horse prior to the eighteenth century resemble a dachshund. It has short legs and a single eye in the middle of its forehead, like a cyclops. The tail is thin and curved and ends in a strange appendage resembling a crescent moon. The hill figure was also the subject of a scouring ritual, which took place from the eighteenth century until 1873, when the horse was restored and outlined in stones.

At least one famous hill figure of a horse has vanished in historical times, and it may be only one of many. This is the Red Horse of Tysoe, which could once be seen about eight miles from the Warwickshire village of Banbury, where the road to Stratford-upon-Avon descends to the Civil War battleground of Edgehill. The Red Horse was allegedly of Saxon date and had been carved in remembrance of Hengist. Unfortunately it was ploughed over sometime in the early 1800s.

The place-name of Tysoe has a pagan origin, for it means 'the land dedicated to Tiw'. He was a Germanic god of war, and it is possible that the Saxons who colonized the area were devotees of a horse cult which was associated with this deity. Tiw or Tyr was also a god of agriculture and gave his name to the English weekday Tuesday.

The Red Horse was accompanied by a smaller figure representing a foal. Local tradition says the Saxons celebrated a festival at the spring equinox (21 March) which was sacred to the Red Horse and Tiw. In more recent times scouring of the hill figure was carried out on Palm Sunday, which may have been a folk-memory of the Saxon rites of spring.

The Uffington, Westbury and Tysoe horses share the area with at least nine other White Horse hill figures. They date from 1778 to as recently as 1937 but, considering the ancient tradition of horse-worship in the area, it is conceivable that some of the older ones were carved on the sites of pagan examples of the genre.

From the White Horses the investigation of hill figures progresses to the giants carved in the landscape. Two of these in particular have become famous in recent years: the Long Man of Wilmington in Sussex and the Cerne Abbas giant in Dorset.

The Long Man is carved on a south-facing slope of Windover Hill, near the village of Wilmington, about three miles from Eastbourne on the Sussex coast. It is around 500 feet above sea-level and can be clearly seen from the road which passes the base of the hill.

The figure has been given various names over the centuries, including the Green Man, the Lone Man and the Lanky Man. It is depicted as a fairly slim, humanoid figure with outstretched arms which hold two staves or poles in each hand. Its present appearance can be accurately dated to 1873 when the Duke of Devonshire paid for the Long Man to be restored after years of neglect, and it was outlined in bricks. In 1925 the ruins of the local Wilmington Priory, whose monks seem to have taken an unusual interest in the hill figure, and the Long Man were taken over by the Sussex Archaeological Trust. It is they, together with the National Trust, who are responsible for its present care and upkeep.

The figure of the Long Man is 231 feet high, while the two staves are 231 and 235 feet high. They are placed approximately 115 feet apart. Whoever designed the Long Man did so with some artistic accuracy, for it is in complete perspective. It is credited as the largest known representation of the human figure in the world.

Theories about the Long Man have always bordered on the sensational. Some archaeologists say the Wilmington giant is of prehistoric origin, while others claim it was carved only in the fourteenth century, by the Benedictine monks of the priory. Rumours had circulated in the Middle Ages that the brothers were practitioners of the magical arts and indulged in heretical or pagan practices. It has been hinted that the priory was a centre for the revival of the Old Religion in the Middle Ages and that this was connected with the hill figure.

Early descriptions of the Long Man link it with fertility or agricultural rites for a good harvest. The earliest description of the figure was in 1779, when apparently the Long Man held a rake and a scythe in its hands. Today the carving is faceless, but as late as 1926 illustrations show it with human features. There is also a local legend that the Long Man once had a cap or helmet – hence the folk ditty 'When Long Man wears his cap, we in the valley get a drop.' Meteorologists say this is only a reference to the fact that when Windover Hill is covered in low cloud a shower of rain can be expected. It seems that, as the hill figure was scoured over the years, its extra features of agricultural tools and a face gradually vanished from view.

The Long Man has been confidently identified as the Norse gods Baldur and Odin, a neolithic god of the harvest, the Saxon super-hero Beowulf, the Greek god Apollo, the Roman deity Mercury and even Mohammed and St Paul! There is a Sussex legend that two giants lived on the downs once upon a time. One dwelt on Windover Hill and the other on Firle Beacon, across the other side of the valley. The giants quarrelled and threw boulders at one another, which created the crater or hollow above the Long Man's head. The Windover giant was killed in this exchange of missiles, and the outline of his body can still be seen today on the hillside.

The vicinity of the long barrow or neolithic burial mound on Windover Hill above the hill figure, known locally as the Giant's Grave in memory of the battling giants, is traditionally a meeting-place for Sussex witches. Doreen Valiente, in her book *Where Witchcraft Lives* (Aquarian Press, 1962), has described a modern witchcraft ritual attended by members of a local coven which took place at this site in the late 1950s. In more recent years both psychic researchers and witches have used the Long Man for magical purposes. This has caused some ill-feeling in the locality, as they have been less than discreet in their activities.

The discovery in 1964 of an Anglo-Saxon cemetery at Finglesham in Kent has lent some credit to the theory that the Wilmington giant is of Saxon origin. Among the objects unearthed in the burial ground was a bronze belt buckle in the shape of a nude male figure wearing a horned cap or helmet

Somerton Maze, Oxfordshire

Entrance stone at Newgrange, Co. Meath

Chalice Well, Glastonbury

Shell Grotto, Grotto Hill, Margate

Chartres Cathedral

Sheela-na-gig at Kilpeck Church, Hereford and Worcester

and carrying two spears in his outstretched hands. This figure has been identified as the shaman god Odin of Norse mythology who was known among the Saxons as Woden. This god was renowned for his magical powers of shapeshifting and for the invention of the magical alphabet known as runes. He was a deity of the wind and the storm and the traditional leader of the Wild Hunt which hunted the souls of the dead on winter nights.

It is possible that the Christian missionaries who converted Sussex, the home of the South Saxons, from paganism and founded Wilmington Abbey found the locals worshipping Odin or Woden. As the monks at the priory were suspected of heresy in the Middle Ages, it may be that this pagan worship continued in the area long after its natives were allegedly weaned from their heathen religion.

The rake and scythe shown in the eighteenth-century drawing, which have prompted the theory that the Long Man was a harvest deity, may be just a red herring. Certainly these features had disappeared by 1850, when a contemporary print shows the hill figure as it is today. Resistivity readings taken in the 1960s do indicate some anomalies which suggest the staves were once longer, and there is a suggestion of a horn-like protuberance on the side of the head.

The other major giant hill figure in the south of England can be found at Cerne Abbas in Dorset. This figure is on Giant Hill, about eight miles west of the market town of Dorchester and a quarter of a mile north-west of the actual village of Cerne Abbas. It can be viewed easily from a layby on the A352 road, and a footpath leads up from the village to the giant, which is under the protection of the National Trust.

Cerne's giant is 180 feet high and forty-five feet across the shoulders. It has a head twenty-four feet in length and waves a club which is 120 feet long. The figure is outlined in graphic detail and is a naked male with ribs and nipples clearly visible and a large erect phallus. There are several similarities between it and the Long Man. Both are carved out on the side of downs which run across southern England, both face south towards the sea, and both have a Benedictine religious house nearby. There is no suggestion that the Sussex giant was ever ithyphallic but the virile nature of the Cerne Abbas hill figure has been his most noted feature over the centuries and a matter of great public interest and, sometimes, censure. For decency's sake the early surveys of the giant omitted his most obvious attribute! Even in modern times there have been isolated calls for his virility to be either covered up or removed completely but thankfully these crankish outcries have been ignored.

The earliest illustration of the giant in all his phallic glory was published in *The Gentleman's Magazine* in 1764. The account with it said that the hill figure was over a thousand years old, and it refers to three letters or numbers, possibly 798, carved between its legs. This odd carving led to fanciful speculation that the giant was meant to represent Jehovah, the Christ or the classical god of time, Saturn.

Local tradition says the outline of the figure was carved around the body of a real giant who in olden times terrorized the area. One night the giant devoured a whole flock of sheep. When he lay down on the hillside to sleep off this little snack, the villagers crept up and killed him. This giant also had a taste for young maidens when he could not find any sheep, and he seriously depleted the flower of local womanhood before he met his end.

Above the hill figure is an ancient rectangular earthworks known as the Frying Pan. This was once the site for a springtime fair held on May Day (Beltane). A fir tree was cut down in the village and carried up the hill on the evening of 30 April. It was erected in the earthworks and was used as a maypole by the villagers next day.

It was alleged the people of the area worshipped serpents and fishes until they were conquered by the Celts, who introduced sun-worship. It was the Celts, so the story goes, who carved the giant, who was their solar god Bel or Belinus. A thirteenth-century tale of the area's conversion to Christianity states that St Augustine visited Cerne Abbas but was driven out of the village by its inhabitants, who pelted him and his disciples with rotting fish tails. An alternative version has Augustine finding the area addicted to the worship of the pagan god Helith. This may be a corruption of the name of the Greek solar god Helios, whose attributes were stolen by the hero Hercules. He carried a large club, so this has led to speculation that the hill figure is meant to be Hercules and is of Romano-British origin. The name Cerne has also been compared with Cernnunos, the Celtic stag god, and the Saxon horned god Herne, who was one of the leaders of the Wild Hunt.

The May Day dancing held in the Frying Pan above the giant may have been a survival of the erotic rites performed by worshippers of the Horned God. A folk-song about the hill figure calls him Beelzebub. This was a common name for the Devil in medieval times. It originated in the names of the Celtic solar god Bel and the Middle Eastern fertility deity Baal, whose worship was condemned by the Old Testament prophets.

The giant's fertility powers were legendary. Until recent times brides-to-be climbed up the hill on the night before their wedding to sleep on the hill figure's phallus. The same custom was carried out by sterile women who desperately wanted to conceive. It is said that one day a nun asked a local the way to the giant. She was told, 'A'iant much use you going up there, m'dear!' The attempts over the years to eradicate his phallic nature have not been well received by local people. They believe that the crops will fail if the Cerne giant is emasculated.

Among the most controversial of the hill figures in Britain are the so-called Gogmagog giants in Cambridgeshire. The story of their rediscovery is a classic detective story of archaeology which illustrates the way Earth Mysteries research, in the face of academic opposition, can utilize local history to recover the lost heritage of our ancient past.

The tale begins in the twelfth century, when Gervase of Tilbury, a writer of fairy tales for the crowned heads of

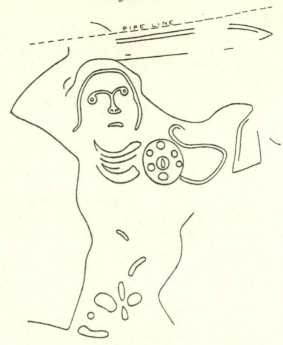

The Warrior God

Europe, included in one of his volumes the strange legend of Wandlebury. This legend tells how a fierce tribe of warriors called the Wandeli camped at the hill-fort of Wandlebury and murdered the local Christians. The Wandeli were presumably Vandals, barbarian mercenaries introduced into Britain by the Romans. Gervase related that anyone who visited the hill-fort on the night of the full moon and cried out 'Knight! Knight!' would be confronted by one of these armed warriors.

Gervase goes on to quote the story of a battle between the ghostly warrior and a young knight called Osbert, son of Hugh. In the fight Osbert is severely wounded in the thigh (a popular euphemism for the sexual organs in medieval times) but manages to capture the warrior's black horse. Unfortunately at cockcrow the horse rides off and is never seen again. Every year on the anniversary of the struggle Osbert's wound splits open and bleeds profusely.

This romantic tale fascinated a local antiquarian, Tom Leth-bridge, who for thirty years was the director of excavations for the Cambridge Antiquarian Society and the University Museum of Ethnology and Archaeology. He was also, more controversially, a dowser and psychic researcher who wrote several books on the subject of ghosts and witchcraft. In 1936 Lethbridge had a letter published in *The Times* on the origin of the name Gogmagog Hills which was used for the area around Wandlebury. He mentioned the tradition that a hill figure, or figures, had once been carved on the side of the hill but had long ago vanished.

The first reference to this figure was in 1605, when it was called a giant by a clerical writer. In 1640 another source said that the meaning of the term Gogmagog could be traced back to a giant heathen image which was once carved in the turf at Wandlebury. In the seventeenth century the figure was appar-ently already in an advanced state of deterioration, although a reference to it in 1724 states it was still visible to the naked eye. The last recorded mention of the giant was in the mid-nineteenth century, and its disappearance after this coincided with the planting of a copse of beech trees on the site.

Although the hill figure had vanished from sight, local folklore kept its memory alive. In the early years of this century children were warned by their parents to keep away from Wandlebury Hill because the bodies of two giants called Gog and Magog were buried there. Another folk-tale said a golden chariot was buried under the nearby Mutlow Hill, which is the site of a Bronze Age burial ground.

Historical references to Gog and Magog can be read in the Bible. Gog is the land of Prince Magog, who is a renowned warrior. Another reference is given by Geoffrey of Monmouth in his *History of Britain* dating from the twelfth century. Geoffrey told his readers that the Ancient Britons were the descendants of Brutus and his Trojans. When the Trojans invaded the British Isles, one of their generals fought a bloody battle with a giant called Gogmagog.

There is evidence that two giant hill figures once existed at Plymouth in Devon, and they were also called Gog and Magog. Local history records the existence of these giants in 1486. In 1529 the figures were cleaned for the princely sum of 8d, but by 1566 the cost had risen to an inflated 20d. Sometime after that date the giants vanished from public view.

In 1954 Lethbridge's continued interest in the mystery of the Wandlebury figure prompted him to take some practical action. This was largely the result of a conversation he had with his museum assistant, who said that as a child he had met an old man who remembered the giant from his own childhood days. In the autumn of 1954 Lethbridge was granted permission by the Cambridge Preservation Society to carry out a preliminary excavation at Wandlebury to try to locate the missing Gogmagog hill figure.

He soon realized that any attempt to use spades or heavy digging-equipment to find the hill figure would in fact destroy it. He decided instead to use a steel bar to probe the chalk topsoil on the hillside and find any odd irregularities under the surface. This was an old method used by local farmers to locate field drains which had become silted up through years of disuse.

The examination of the hillside by the Cambridge archaeologist was meticulous. Using sticks, he plotted each day's soundings and recorded their pattern each evening in a notebook. By the end of the first week of investigation Lethbridge had already achieved results. A shape had begun to take form but it was difficult to identify it. He sent a tracing of it to a friend who worked at the British Museum. The reply came back by return of post that the shape was the rear end of an animal, possibly a horse. Subsequent soundings exposed the figure as a woman mounted on a horse. The length of the figure was calculated at 104 feet from nose to tail.

The excavation had set out to find a giant, who was possibly the representation of the ancient warrior in the legend, but instead found the carving of a woman with goggle eyes, long flowing hair and large breasts, seated on a horse. At first, in

The Mother Goddess

the early stages, Lethbridge thought he had located the image of a Roman cavalryman until its breasts were uncovered. He then tentatively identified the figure as the Celtic horse goddess Epona who was generally associated with the White Horses.

Naturally Lethbridge was excited to have discovered a hill figure but surprised and puzzled to have found a female goddess rather than the male giant he had been expecting. He therefore decided to continue the excavations, believing that the giant mentioned in local folklore still existed. Over the next few weeks he extended his plotting, and gradually another figure began to take shape near the hind legs of the

The Sun God

goddess' horse. At first Lethbridge thought it was just an extension of the horse's legs but then he realized it was a cart or chariot attached to the animal by a shaft. This new discovery seemed to justify the legend of the chariot buried nearby. .

Working on, Lethbridge found the figure of a second

human form. To do this he had to cut back a wilderness of briars, small thorn trees and elm suckers which had covered the site for years. What he found was well worth this physical exertion. It was a giant hooded warrior carrying a short Roman-style sword and a round shield of Celtic or Saxon design.

When Lethbridge probed above the head of the female figure, he uncovered a crescent moon, which told him she was a lunar deity. This was an interesting revelation, for local people around Uffington in Berkshire had always called the White Horse there 'the moon stallion'. White mares had been identified with the Great Mother Goddess who was one of the aspects of the triple goddess worshipped by the Celts.

Working outwards from the two figures, Lethbridge began to plot a new shape, which was eventually revealed as the strange-looking image of a hunchbacked man wearing a cowled robe. This figure was 117 feet high and eighty-five feet wide. It had been executed in a flowing artistic style which Lethbridge thought resembled Celtic art forms.

The excavations at Wandlebury had exposed three huge hill figures, not the single one mentioned in the medieval accounts. They were a goddess, a warrior and a giant. But what were their purpose and meaning?

Lethbridge accepted the idea that the first figure of a naked woman was the goddess Epona or some older deity who was the patron of white horses and the moon. He further believed that this goddess had been the object of worship by the Celtic tribe of the Iceni who had occupied the Cambridge area in the Iron Age. He was of the opinion that the Celts might have taken over the worship of this goddess from the indigenous people of the region. To them she was the archetypal Great Mother, who was known as Magog. Lethbridge pointed out that in the Indo-European language *Ma* means 'mother'. In modern India the prefix *maha* is 'great', as in *mahatma*, 'great soul', a title given to Hindu holy men.

The hooded, hunchbacked figure was, according to Lethbridge, a solar god who was the consort of the Great

Mother Goddess. He and the warrior figure may have been later additions to the hill carving, as originally it was the goddess who was the principal object of veneration in the local religion.

Lethbridge seems to have been uncertain about the identity of the warrior figure. He was eventually to decide it represented Wandil, an ancient giant god of death, darkness and the underworld. This god had given his name to the hill-fort where the figures had been found.

The three deities of Wandlebury symbolized the mystical powers of light, fertility and darkness worshipped by our pagan ancestors. There were stories of orgiastic revels held at Wandlebury in medieval times. A Tudor edict expressly forbids students from Cambridge University to attend these orgies. Ceremonies of this type would have been held in the spring to acknowledge the victory of the forces of light (summer) over the powers of darkness (winter), symbolized on the Wandlebury hillside by the hunchbacked solar god and the hooded warrior. Rites of death and rebirth would have been held in the autumn, when the dark tide began to flow, signifying the beginning of winter. The rituals performed by the worshipper of the Wandlebury gods would have coincided with the Celtic religious festivals of Beltane in May and Samhain in October.

Amateur archaeologist, Christian O'Brien, believes that the Wandlebury earthwork was used as a lunar observatory by ancient astronomer priests. From his investigations he has dated the earthwork and its alignments to 2,500 BCE. He has put forward the theory that the sun god of the Wandlebury hill figures was the Celtic deity Ogma, who invented writing and the arts of civilization. It is obvious from both Lethbridge's and O'Brien's work that Wandlebury is a very important site, providing evidence of the beliefs and practices of ancient religion, but official recognition of this fact has not been forthcoming.

Not all of Lethbridge's academic colleagues were as convinced as he was that his excavations had uncovered a row of Celtic or pre-Celtic gods carved on the Wandlebury hillside. His findings were dismissed as a freak and, because he had shown an interest in psychic research and witchcraft, he was dismissed as an eccentric and a crank. The Cambridge Preservation Society lost interest in the project once the investigation began to produce tangible results, and the neglect of the site as the controversy raged led to the serious degradation of the uncovered hill figures.

In 1969 and 1970 an attempt was made by a group of students from the university to restore the site to the state of preservation in which Lethbridge had left it. By this time the area had become overgrown once again and the face of the goddess image could barely be seen. In 1978 representatives of the Cambridge-based Institute for Geomantic Research approached the local preservation society and asked their permission to scour the hill figures. They were allowed to do this providing no actual fresh digging work was carried out at the site. Agreement was reached on this point, a starting-date was fixed and work commenced. Shortly afterwards the society changed their mind. They advised the institute that the scouring could not be allowed unless a resistivity survey was carried out by the university's Department of Archaeology. This survey was to establish the exact position of the hill figures and their correct outline. A suggestion by the IGR that the site should be fenced off to protect the figures and prevent any further damage was rejected by the society.

Today the Gogmagog figures lie neglected and overgrown, remembered only by the dedicated band of Earth Mysteries students who are sympathetic to our ancient heritage. It is a national scandal that these sacred images, no less important than the Uffington White Horse, the Long Man and the Cerne giant, should have been allowed to fade back into the historical obscurity from which Lethbridge rescued them in the 1950s.

A story similar to that of the rediscovery of the Wandlebury gods surrounds the Giant of Penhill in Wensleydale, Yorkshire. This lost hill figure was rediscovered recently by Ian Taylor, who was following up clues into folk-traditions

and legends relating to the area. The legend of Penhill told of a
giant, who was the son of the Norse thunder god Thor, living in
the locality, who terrified the country people. He owned an
equally massive hound called Wolfshead, which he accidentally
shot with an arrow. When the giant's pet boar was killed, he
ordered the locals to bring their youngest sons to him so he
could wreak revenge. If nobody owned up to the killing, the
giant said he would kill all the children. Fortunately for all
concerned, the ogre was confronted by a hermit with magical
powers, his castle was burned down and he was chased by the
spectral form of his dead hound until he fell over a cliff and
died.

This bizarre tale led Ian Taylor to investigate the old stories
of the giants of Albion mentioned by Geoffrey of Monmouth.
He also traced the name Penhill back to the Celtic or Welsh
prefix *Pen*, meaning 'head' or 'chief'. It is his theory that the
legend of the giant of Penhill mingles Celtic and Saxon
elements. Although the giant was kin to the Norse god Thor,
Taylor believes he could also have been connected with the
Germanic sky god Woden (Odin in Norse myth), the Scandinavian fertility god Frey and the Celtic solar god Bel or Belinus.
In Taylor's theory, the hermit stands for the new faith of
Christianity defeating the Old Gods of the pagan religion.

Taylor further links the giant with a folk-custom still carried
out each August in the nearby village of Wilton, called 'Burning
the Bartle'. This ritual consists of carrying an effigy, known as
the Bartle, through the village streets and then setting it alight.
The custom allegedly commemorates the hunting-down of a
sheep thief in the sixteenth century, but Taylor rejects this
notion, claiming instead that the legend and the folk-custom are
derived from the Celtic and pre-Celtic worship of a solar god
which was celebrated in the vicinity of a lost hill figure carved at
Penhill. He has suggested that the Cerne giant, the Long Man
and the Penhill giant are all symbols of solar power and were
objects of worship in pagan fertility rites involving magical
weather-control to produce a good harvest.

In his researches Taylor links the supposed hill figure at

Penhill with a series of astronomical alignments in the area. These alignments, he claims, are connected with various megalithic monuments in the vicinity of the giant and have a lunar, solar and stellar significance. It is therefore evident that the worship of the deity represented by the legend of the Penhill giant may date back to the megalithic culture.

Our examination of hill figures has concentrated on White Horses and giants, but there are other carvings in the landscape which are worthy of attention, even if they are more abstract in conception. Two examples of this type fall into the category, and these are the Bledlow and Whiteleaf Crosses which can be seen in the Chilterns.

The Bledlow Cross is on the north-west slope of Wain Hill, about a mile from the village of Chinnor in Buckinghamshire. It is close to the ancient trackway known as the Icknield Way which was originally a neolithic green road and also passes the White Horse at Uffington.

The cross is equal-armed, which is a pagan sign pre-dating the coming of Christianity to these parts. In ancient religious and magical traditions the equal-armed cross represented the sun and the elemental forces of fire, earth, air and water. Locally the Bledlow Cross is said to have healing powers, for if you run across it barefoot, you will be filled with energy. This may be a heavily guarded reference to the revitalizing properties of the Earth energy found at natural power centres.

Its neighbour, the Whiteleaf Cross, is to be found on a steep side of the Chilterns facing west over the Vale of Aylesbury near Monks Risborough and about thirty miles from Uffington. It is an unbalanced, Calvary cross surmounted on a pyramid and situated just below a neolithic burial mound.

Both the crosses have been claimed as pre-Christian phallic symbols carved in connection with the pagan fertility rites practised by the ancients. Their date is unknown but at least one archaeologist claims that their dimensions are based on a sacred measurement of 11.61 inches which is common to both Stonehenge and the Long Man of Wilmington. At present the origin and true purpose of these symbols are a riddle.

One of the most amazing landscape figures to have been discovered in recent years is the Sussex Elephant. While this is not a hill figure, it does not really fit into the category of terrestrial zodiacs either, so it will be included in this chapter. The elephant was revealed in the early 1980s by an Earth Mysteries researcher, Mike Collier. He claims that the huge terrestrial image of the elephant covers an area measuring 3½ miles by three miles. It faces due west and can be found approximately 4½ miles west of the popular Sussex seaside resort of Eastbourne.

The animal is outlined by roads, footpaths and parish boundaries and would appear to be a representation in the landscape of the English countryside of a young elephant of the Asian species. Its front foot stands a mile from the Long Man of Wilmington; its outline includes the Roman road which travels from Lewes to Pevensey; the River Cuckmere flows directly out of its mouth, and its eye is formed by an island around which flow a river and a stream. Michelham Priory, a thirteenth-century religious house, is just above the elephant's head, while a footpath lining the priory with the church of St Pancras at Arlington forms the outline of its ear. This church is of Norman origin but is on the site of an earlier Saxon edifice which may have been built on pagan foundations.

The area of the tusk near the church is formed by an earthwork which is concreted on one side and was built by the Eastbourne Waterworks Company in the 1960s. Collier speculates that this was built over an earlier earthwork. However, they advised him that this was not so but informed him that during the excavations the tusk of a prehistoric mammoth had been dug up!

Why a figure of an elephant should appear in the English countryside has yet to be adequately explained. It is known that carvings of elephants have been found on the site of a pre-Christian round tower in Scotland, so their existence was recognized here. It is possible that some elephants – African rather than Asian – were imported by the Romans, and there may have been racial memories still extant of the woolly mammoths which used to roam the forests of Ice Age Europe. Collier seems to regard the elephant as the surviving remnant of a lost terrestrial zodiac, but no evidence has so far been found to back up this idea.

It is certain that the hill figures of southern England were an attempt by the ancient people who carved them to bring the old gods down to Earth. By symbolically representing these deities on the land, their worshippers hoped to transfer the gods' divine power from heaven into the locality in which they were carved. These figures became the focus of powerful rituals designed to unlock the geomantic forces which permeated the landscape and were symbolized by the sacred images carved in the hillsides.

5

EARTH ZODIACS
AND
MAZES

One of the speculative aspects of Earth Mysteries is the subject of terrestrial or Earth zodiacs. The concept of huge figures in the landscape representing the signs of the zodiac has captured the public imagination. Earth zodiacs obviously have an astrological origin. In the past twenty years astrology has experienced a revival. Unfortunately, as with all populist revivals of this kind, the subject has become trivialized. While nearly every daily newspaper and weekly women's magazine publishes an astrological column or feature, the predictions provided, based only on the generalized sun signs, cannot be individually precise. To produce a detailed forecast or character analysis, the astrologer has to set up a birth chart for the person concerned. Astrological articles in newspapers and magazines may be fun, but they are not an example of genuine astrology.

Astrology developed from the observation of the stars by early astronomer priests and from the occult knowledge of the initiates of the Ancient Wisdom who were in contact with stellar influences. At first astrology and religion were united in a spiritual philosophy which, while centred on our planet, also embraced other star systems beyond our own. Gradually the religious aspects of astrology were neglected and, at its popular level, it degenerated into a superstitious belief.

In a previous chapter it has been explained how the stone circles and standing stones were aligned to the stars and constellations. The ancients knew of the stellar influences emanating from the heavens which affected life on Earth. Astrology, the study of these stellar and planetary influences, is a cosmic science which provides a way of interpreting the patterns in the universe which are also discernible through the application of spiritual geometry.

The development of astrology from the early astronomical observations of the ancients can be dated to approximately 3,000 BCE. During the time of the Sumerian culture, which arose in the Middle East around this period, the constellations were identified with archetypal images in the form of animals. By 2,500 BCE an astrologically based religion had developed in Ancient Egypt, embracing pyramid-building, the worship of the star Sirius, and priest astronomers who formed a powerful political and spiritual elite in Egyptian society. Their hierophant (high priest) wore a ritual cloak of spotted panther skin which represented the starry night sky, ruled over Heliopolis, the City of the Sun, and was known by the title Chief Astrologer. These astrologer priests usurped the role of the ancient clan of priestesses who were initiates of the stellar wisdom.

At the same period a complex civilization arose in the Far East and occupied the Indus valley of India. This culture was to have a profound effect on the history of astrology. The Indus people traded with the Middle East and exported the ancient Indian system of astrology based on either six or eight zodiac signs depicted in animal form. In the Indus city of Mohenjodaro have been found seals of the horned god known as the Lord of the Animals. This ithyphallic deity sits crosslegged surrounded by jungle beasts and has been regarded as the Eastern prototype of the Celtic stag god, Cernnunos.

By 1500 BCE astrology was well established in the Middle East, especially in Babylonia and Chaldea. It was during this period that the ziggurats (pyramid temples) were built for astronomical observation, astrological divination and star-worship. Between 1500 and 500 BCE the Chaldeans' astrological expertise was exported to many other countries. The twelve signs of the zodiac we recognize today came into prominence at this time and are a combination of Chaldean, Egyptian, Arabic, Chinese and Indian stellar lore.

Astrology divides the human race into twelve personality types, depending upon the month of the year they were born in, and on the zodiac sign the sun was passing through at the time. These birth signs are represented symbolically by an animal, human or abstract image as follows:

> Aries the Ram (21 March – 20 April)
> Taurus the Bull (21 April – 20 May)
> Gemini the Twins (21 May – 20 June)
> Cancer the Crab (21 June – 20 July)
> Leo the Lion (21 July – 21 August)
> Virgo the Virgin (22 August – 22 September)
> Libra the Scales (23 September – 22 October)
> Scorpio the Scorpion (23 October – 22 November)
> Sagittarius the Archer (23 November – 20 December)
> Capricorn the Goat (21 December – 19 January)
> Aquarius the Water-Bearer (20 January – 18 February)
> Pisces the Fishes (19 February – 20 March)

Different cultures have alternative forms for the zodiac images but in general the above symbols are recognized by most astrologers. It will be obvious from these divisions of the signs that the zodiac is linked with the solstices and the equinoxes, marked by change-over dates of specific signs, and the phases of the moon which passes through each of the zodiac signs during its monthly cycle.

The Earth zodiac is a grouping of the astrological signs of effigies which can be detected in the natural or artificial features of the landscape. The theory is that either the ancients actually changed the geophysical features of the land to create these huge images or they were in some unknown way imposed on the geography of their locale by cosmic forces. In general the Earth zodiacs can be viewed properly only from the air, which has predictably led to considerable sensational speculation as to their origins and purpose.

The first terrestrial zodiac to be discovered in modern times was at Glastonbury in the 1920s. This find was the work of Katherine Maltwood, who had been studying an Ordnance Survey map of the area when she noticed that the contours of the River Cary near Glastonbury resembled the underside of a lion. She eventually traced the complete outline of the lion on the map and found it was at least three miles long. The outline was formed by ancient roads, footpaths, ditches, streams and earthworks. Maltwood identified the animal as the astrological lion, Leo, and she went on to locate the other zodiac signs forming what she called 'the Temple of the Stars' in the Somerset countryside.

To begin with, the Glastonbury Zodiac was regarded as a 'one-off', but in recent years other examples have been found at Nuthampstead in Hertfordshire, Pendle in Lancashire, Kingston-on-Thames in Surrey, and Pumpsaint and Preseli in West Wales. Each of these zodiacs has its own unique features but all are based on the traditional astrological signs, even if their imagery does appear to differ in subtle ways.

Glastonbury, probably because it was the first to be discovered, is still the most famous of the Earth zodiacs. It was, as we have seen, a sacred power centre in pre-Christian Britain. The Celts regarded it as one of the entrances to the Otherworld; Arthurian legend cites it as the mythical Avalon and the dwelling-place of the sorceress Morgan le Fay, whose nine acolytes guarded the holy well at Chalice Hill. In the Christian era the Goddess-worship of pagan times was sublimated in the reverence of the Blessed Virgin Mary by the early Church.

Katherine Maltwood believed the Glastonbury Zodiac had been created as early as 2,700 BCE by Sumerian astrologers who had visited Britain. The zodiac, which covers an area ten miles in diameter around the Somerset town, survived to the present day because allegedly the local inhabitants consciously or unconsciously followed the contours of its effigies when they laid out new roads and footpaths and made agricultural improvements. This argument had been challenged by orthodoxy, and it is true that, due to a lack of hard evidence about events thousands of years ago, many aspects of terrestrial zodiac research have to be a matter of faith.

Maltwood, and the other zodiac researchers who followed her lead, used mythology and folklore to provide the evidence to support her astonishing discovery. This process is, of course, a legitimate one and in Earth Mysteries research can provide startling results, as in the uncovering of the Wandlebury hill figures. Although Maltwood was convinced the Glastonbury Zodiac was of Sumerian origin, she also became convinced that it encapsulated in its images and mythic tradition the matter of the Arthurian cycle of legends, including the quest for the Holy Grail. The majority of these legends are a product of medieval romance but the original versions had roots in the Celtic or pre-Celtic religions.

The word Somerset was derived by Maltwood from the term 'Seat of the Sumers' or Sumerians. Their capital was, she alleged, the present site of the town of Somerton, whose name echoes their cultural influence. She also claimed that the word 'somersault', which the *Oxford English Dictionary* says derives from the Latin *supra*, 'above', and *saltus*, 'leap', was a reference to the turning wheel of the zodiac in the English countryside.

Mary Caine, who in the 1960s and 1970s followed up Maltwood's research and also discovered the new zodiac at Kingston-on-Thames, believes that the twelve hides of land granted to Joseph of Arimathea and his twelve disciples by the Druids are evidence that these early Christians knew the secret of the Glastonbury Zodiac. According to Bligh Bond's spirit guide, the fifteenth-century monk known as Johannes, a replica of a zodiac was once carved on the chapel floor inside Glastonbury Abbey.

The medieval abbey was often known as 'the secret of the Lord' from the persistent legend that Joseph had buried the Grail within its precincts. Both Maltwood and Caine claim that the 'Grail' was in fact the Earth zodiac in the surrounding countryside. Maltwood saw the Round Table of Arthurian myth as the astrological zodiac, with its twelve knights symbolizing each sign. Sir George Trevalyn and Edward Matchett, two writers on New Age themes, have also put forward this suggestion. They compare Arthur with the sun and designate the knights as representatives of the zodiac signs. In many of the legends of Arthur with a Celtic flavour, the warrior king has all the attributes of a solar god. Painton Ewen, a modern authority on medieval rose windows, has described stained glass depictions in French churches of the Christ as a symbolic sun encircled by the signs of the zodiac.

Mary Caine identifies King Arthur in the Glastonbury Zodiac with Sagittarius the Archer. In the Somerset zodiac this astrological sign is represented by a centaur. The figure is over five miles long and is bordered by Catsham and Battonsbough in the north, Ponters Ball in the east, Arthur's Bridge in the west and West Pennard in the south. The name Battonsbough is derived by Caine from the Middle Eastern fertility deity Baal, worshipped by the Phoenicians, who traded for tin in Cornwall. In ancient times the worship of Baal was widespread in the West Country, and he was identified with the Celtic solar god Bel. Caine also identifies Arthur with the Assyrian sun god Ahura, who was said by ancient astrologers to rule the constellation of Sagittarius.

The centaur used to depict Sagittarius in the Glastonbury Zodiac was a mythological beast who, it is believed, was derived from the first garbled sightings of warriors on horseback, who appeared to be joined to their mounts. Caine links the centaur with St George, the patron saint of England, who in Judeo-Christian myth slew the dragon. This creature was regarded as a symbol of the Devil but also of the Earth energy which flows along the ley lines between ancient power centres. Arthur, St George and St Michael have always been linked in popular folk-tradition and religious belief.

In the Glastonbury Zodiac Capricorn is depicted in its traditional form as a goat. Its back is formed by the Glastonbury–Shepton Mallet road; its head and single horn are in the region of Ponter's Ball, while its cloven hoofs touch Launcherley Hill and Barrow at the rear and Fountain's Wall at the front. This effigy's single horn led Caine to think it might really be a unicorn rather than a goat. In occult lore the unicorn is a symbol of the moon goddess and sexual polarity. A rather suggestive legend claims that the wild unicorn can be tamed only if it 'lays its head in the lap of a virgin'. This suggests a cryptic reference to the power of female sexuality to control masculine energy.

The sign of Capricorn was historically significant to the heretical Order of the Knights Templar. They reputedly worshipped an androgynous deity, Baphomet, who had a goat's head and legs but the torso and arms of a human being. In the esoteric tradition, the Capricorn goat which climbs the sacred mountain is a symbol of the initiate reaching for spiritual perfection. Glastonbury Tor is an example of the sacred mountain in the British landscape.

Templar symbols can be found carved on old houses in the village of Wick, at the nose of the Capricorn effigy. Nearby are two ancient oaks nicknamed Gog and Magog, symbols of the sun god and the Great Mother Goddess. At the nearby, strangely named Paradise, the Templars are associated with a holy well. In Earth Mysteries lore holy wells and sacred springs were dedicated to the Goddess and were regarded as places of initiation and oracular wisdom. The Templars are traditionally regarded as the guardians of both the Holy Grail and the geomantic tradition handed down from pagan times. It is not surprising that they should be found near Glastonbury and its Earth zodiac.

The sign of Aquarius in the Glastonbury Zodiac deviates from its usually known form of the human water-carrier and is an eagle or phoenix. The effigy is about half a mile across and contains both the Tor and Chalice Hill, with its sacred well. In fact, its beak rests on the well, confirming the reputation of the phoenix as a motif of regeneration. The eagle has also been granted attributes of healing in ancient mythology. In Ancient Egypt the phoenix was the ruler of the seasonal calendar and presided over the celebration of New Year as a symbol of death and rebirth.

Pisces in the zodiac is symbolized by a whale and two fishes. The image covers Wearyall Hill, where Joseph planted his staff when he arrived in Glastonbury, and the coincidentally named Fishers Hill. Some Earth Mysteries researchers have compared this 'whale' with the Celtic salmon of wisdom. In the Arthurian legends the Fisher King is the ruler of the wasteland. The king has been wounded 'in the thigh', and his land is laid waste with famine and death. Only when the Grail is gained by a pure knight can the king be healed and the Wasteland recover. This myth refers to the ancient priest kings who ruled over the land with geomantic wisdom. The fish is also the sign of the Christ, who is the spiritual teacher of the Piscean Age.

A hornless ram represents Aries in the zodiac, and this has been interpreted as a lamb. It was a symbol used by the Templars, and at Bridgewater in Somerset an image of a lamb holding a banner was unearthed on land which had belonged to the order in the Middle Ages. The Arian effigy is made up of the routes of old trackways in the area of Walton and Street. This area has megalithic remains, including two standing stones at Ivythorn near the ram/lamb's front hoofs. Today at Street there exists a factory manufacturing sheepskin coats – an odd coincidence.

From the ram of Aries we come to Taurus the Bull, whose head and back are outlined by Ivythorn Hill and Collard Hill, Castlebrook and Redlands. In the astrological tradition of the great Zodiac Ages, each lasting 2,000 years, the epoch of

Taurus included the Bronze Age, the megalithic period and the pyramid-builders. In this Zodiac Age agriculture was established, the first cities were built and bull-worship was widespread. In astrological terms, Taurus represents the earthly qualities of Mother Earth. However, in the religion of Mithraism, which originated in the Manichean heresy practised by the Templars and the Cathars, the solar god Mithras slays the cosmic bull, and its blood fertilizes the earth. Bull-worship was associated with early agriculture, fertility rites and ritual sacrifice to propitiate the geomantic forces of the land.

Gemini, the sign of the Twins, can be traced next to Taurus, covering Lollover Hill, Castlebrook and Dundun Camp, an Iron Age hill-fort once used as a beacon hill. Caine regards it as a sacred place of spiritual illumination connected with Taliesin, the radiant-browed wizard of myth who was born from Ceridwen's cauldron of inspiration, which was the pagan prototype of the Grail. Astrologically Gemini is the dual aspects of the self, the dark and the light, which are integrated at the end of the Grail quest. Medieval heretics claimed Jesus had a twin brother, and this belief may have been known to the Templars.

In the Glastonbury Zodiac, the sign of Cancer appears as a ship. This seems unusual but Cancer is ruled by the element of water and the moon. In Celtic, Egyptian and Hebrew mythology an important role is played by the sacred boat or ship. Both Isis and Ceridwen are shown travelling in an ark or sacred vessel, and at the end of his life Arthur is carried to Avalon on a boat accompanied by the three queens who are representatives of the triple moon goddess.

From watery Cancer, the zodiac progressed to Leo the Lion, whose symbol conjures up images of royalty and sun-worship. The leonine effigy is three miles long and is outlined by the River Cary in the south and Somerton Lane in the north. His chest is defined by an ancient road, and earthworks form his chin. His eye is marked by Copley wood. The lion has always been a royal animal and is known as 'the

king of the beasts' but was officially accepted in Britain only
by the Normans, who introduced his heraldic image from
France in the eleventh century.

Virgo follows Leo and is the virgin aspect of the triple moon
goddess of the pagan Old Religion. The effigy at Glastonbury
is four miles in length and is crossed by the green road of the
Fosse Way. It covers the area between Wheathill in the north
and Yeovilton in the south. To the east lies the Iron Age
hill-fort of Cadbury Castle, the site of Camelot in the
Arthurian legends.

Mary Caine identifies Virgo with the pagan Earth Mother,
pointing out that the zodiacal effigy is in the vicinity of Annis
Hill. In Celtic mythology Annis is the dark aspect of the
Goddess, while in Christianity she is St Anne, mother of the
Virgin Mary, who is said to have been a British princess.
Wimble Toot is also on the Virgo effigy, and 'toot', or 'tot', is
a name associated with beacon hills as ley-markers and the
symbolic breasts of the Earth goddess.

In the Glastonbury Zodiac the next sign is Libra, which
appears as a dove. It is nearly two miles long and encompasses
Hurtle Pool, Tootle Bridge, Gosling Street and Barton St
Davids. The identification with Libra of the dove is explained
by the fact that the astrological sign is ruled by the planet
Venus, and the dove is associated with the goddess of love.
The bird has also been linked with various heretical
movements, including the Gnostics, who practised a blend of
Christianity and enlightened paganism. In Christian belief the
dove is a symbol of the Holy Spirit and is featured in the
baptism of Jesus as the Christ by John the Baptist, who was a
member of the sect of Essenes.

Scorpio follows Libra and is in the Earth zodiac in its
traditional form as a scorpion. It is also crossed by the Fosse
Way and is bordered by Parbrook in the north, Lattisham in
the west, Hornblotten in the east and Alford in the south.
Astrologically, Scorpio is a watery sign ruled by Pluto, who in
classical mythology was the god of the underworld. The sign
rules sexuality and death, those taboo subjects seldom

discussed in polite company. Glastonbury, as we know, has Otherworld connections, and there is a strong element of death and rebirth in the legends around it.

At Alford in the south of Scorpio, the parish church has a carving of a dragon on one of its pew ends. Other carvings in the church depict a pelican (identified by Mary Caine with the sign of Aquarius), a Templar lamb (Aries?), a Green Man (seen by Caine as a solar deity) and animal symbols of the four evangelists, which are a bull (Taurus), a lion (Leo), an eagle (Scorpio/Aquarius) and a man (Gemini). The church also has a Tau cross entwined with a serpent, which was a symbol used by initiates of the ancient wisdom to signify the union of the male and female principles.

The last effigy in the Glastonbury Zodiac is not an astrological sign but is no less significant from a mystical viewpoint. It is known as the Great Dog of Langport and has its snout resting on Michells (Michael's?) Burrow, its chest outlined by the River Parrett and its tail on the oddly named but very apt village of Wagg. Dogs have been seen as messengers between the gods and the mortal world. Examples include the jackal-headed god Anubis in Ancient Egypt, who guides the soul of the dead to the underworld, the Greek three-headed dog Cerberus, who guards the gates of Hades, and the demonic hounds of the Wild Hunt in Celtic myth, who hunt the spirits of the departed. At Glastonbury the Wild Hunt rides out from the tor on winter nights led by the Celtic god of the underworld, Gwynn ap Nudd. At Cadbury Castle the Wild Hunt is led by Arthur himself. Symbolically therefore the Great Dog of Langport is the guardian of the Glastonbury Zodiac.

Following her researches into the Somerset zodiac effigies, Mary Caine discovered that it was not unique: similar images could be found in the Surrey landscape around the town of Kingston-on-Thames. This zodiac is similar to the one at Glastonbury and covers a large area of east and south Surrey and west London, from Egham in the west and Ealing in the north to Wimbledon in the east and Epsom in the south.

The Kingston Zodiac is regarded as more controversial than its Glastonbury counterpart, possibly because it is situated in a landscape which has been subject to considerably more geographic change. Mary Caine, however, remains convinced that the zodiac is a reality and argues that the changes have subconsciously incorporated imagery and myth which can still be detected today. In fact, it was her realization that public-house names in the Kingston area had astrological meanings which triggered her quest to find an Earth zodiac in its environs.

Kingston has a long history and was once the Saxon capital of south-east England. Hence its name is derived from the ancient king's stone used in coronation ceremonies by the Saxons. This royal connection is also found in the sign of Leo which is close to Hampton Court, used by Henry VIII, who destroyed Glastonbury Abbey. The land around Hampton Court was also owned by the Templars, who seem to be linked with terrestrial zodiacs, and the maze at the royal palace may have been their handiwork.

Virgo covers Nonsuch Park, which was a favourite haunt for the Virgin Queen, Elizabeth I. This zodiac sign also includes Old Malden, whose medieval abbot founded a college at Oxford which has a famous illustration of the astrological signs. Carshalton Ponds is also in Virgo and boasts a statue of Anne Boleyn. Caine regards the six-fingered witch wife of Henry VIII as a human incarnation of Annis and St Anne, who are both to be found in the Glastonbury Zodiac.

Libra, as in the Somerset effigies, pops up at Kingston as the dove. As the symbol of the Word of God, Caine connects it with the many schools and colleges built in the area to educate the masses. After Libra comes Scorpio, the sign of death, sexuality and rebirth. Near it are Robin Hood's Lane and Arthur road, both named for divine kings who died sacrificial deaths in true Scorpionic tradition. Robin died at the hands of a wicked abbess who bled him to death, while Arthur was betrayed by his best friend and met a heroic end at the final battle with his dark son Mordred. Real Scorpio melodrama!

There are also the sites of ancient battles on the effigy and reports of royal deaths in the area.

In the Kingston Zodiac, Sagittarius is still remembered in the Royal Horse Show, the horse-riders in Richmond Park and the polo ponies which frequent yuppy Surrey. In the fifteenth century Richmond Park was a favourite hunting-ground for the Tudor monarchs. Capricorn in the zodiac has the same single horn as the Glastonbury 'unicorn'. It covers Brentford's Goat Wharf, Horn Lane in Acton and Mortlake, where the Elizabethan astrologer and Rosicrucian Dr John Dee lived. Dee is known to have had secret knowledge of 'a great treasure' at Glastonbury, which could have been the zodiac.

Aquarius the Water-Carrier, symbol of the New Age, is the phoenix/eagle in this zodiac; its head is formed by a lake at Osterley which is a bird sanctuary, and it has a place called The Aviary on one of its wings. The Templars also had an influence in the area, founding a hospice in 1106 on the site of the Ostrich Inn in Bath Road. Pisces follows Aquarius in the Heston district. Inside its boundary is the Norman church of Harlington, with a statue of St Peter holding a Bible which has a fish as a bookmark.

Aries the Ram ruled by Mars, the god of war, is centred on Hounslow and is criss-crossed by Roman roads used to transport troops during the occupation of Celtic Britain. Powder Mill Lane on this zodiac effigy was the site of factories supplying gunpowder to the British Army. This area is another Templar stronghold and reminds us that one of their symbols was the Lamb of God, the hornless ram of the Glastonbury Zodiac.

In the Kingston Zodiac, Taurus is a leaping bull of Cretan design. He covers Hampton Court, with its maze, which could be of Templar origin and a copy of the famous Cretan labyrinth where the Minotaur, half bull and half human, was slain by Theseus. Gemini and Cancer cover the region around Molesley. One of the Twins Mary Caine identifies with the legendary giant Atlas, who gave his name to the lost continent

of Atlantis believed by many occultists to have been a source
of geomantic wisdom which arrived in ancient Britain when
Atlantean colonists fled the destruction of their motherland.
The second Twin, she says, could be the Roman god of fire,
Vulcan, whose Norse equivalent was Wayland the Smith of
Uffington fame.

The River Thames forms the outline of Cancer, and Caine
notes that the old name for this river is Tamiesis or Isis, from
the spring which is its source in the Cotswolds beyond Oxford.
Isis was the Ancient Egyptian Mother Goddess who travelled
in her sacred moon boat between this world and the next.
Statues of Isis suckling her son Horus became the model for
medieval images of the Virgin Mary and the baby Jesus.

As at Glastonbury, the Surrey Zodiac has its guard-dog,
whose effigy can be traced in the contours of the landscape
between Egham and Chertsey. Here Cerberus, the canine
watchdog of the underworld, is found at St Anne's Hill,
named after the mother of the Virgin Mary and the Celtic hag
goddess, which had a holy well, an illustration of the saint
with two dogs and a public house nearby with a druidic name.
In recent years the hill became the scene of seasonal rites
practised by a group of neo-Druids. It is not far from Windsor,
where Herne the Hunter rides through the royal park with his
pack of spectral hounds.

In the 1940s Lewis Edwards, the former political agent to
the first Labour prime minister, Ramsay MacDonald,
published details of a 'Welsh Temple of the Stars', which he
had found in his native Carmarthenshire using Ordnance
Survey maps of the area. The Welsh zodiac covered the region
in a diameter of 5½ miles and included the towns of Ffarmers,
Pumpsaint and Lampeter. It has been commonly called the
Pumpsaint Zodiac after the place where five Celtic saints were
buried.

According to Edwards, the centre of this terrestrial zodiac is
south-west of Ffarmers. In a position north-east of this centre
can be found the image of a man on a horse who is Sagittarius
the Archer. This image is marked by the contours of a hill,

and opposite it, nearer the centre, the outline of another hill forms the head of a bull representing Taurus.

A road leading from an inn on Taurus towards Lampeter forms the distinct outline of a ram for Aries. Edwards says the district is called Ram in the English language, and there is a public house of the same name in the locality. The back of the Arian ram is created by an old Roman road leading from Lampeter to Carmarthen. Above Aries are some ancient woodlands which form the sign of Pisces and contain an Iron Age hill-fort and a stone circle.

To the north of the Pumpsaint Zodiac can be found a hill whose Welsh name means 'the hill of the sacred place'. Roads around the hill and a stream to the south side of it produce the figure of a squirrel which Edwards regards as Aquarius. Capricorn lies between this Aquarian tree rodent and Sagittarius and is formed by a hill known locally as Craig Twrch. The goat is a unicorn, as at Glastonbury and Kingston, and at the tip of its single horn is a place known as 'the front of the horn'.

Scorpio can be found in the hills south of the River Cothi in an outline created by the edge of an ancient wood. In this Welsh zodiac Scorpio is a composite symbol made up of a serpent, scorpion and eagle, which is a glyph for the various attributes of the astrological sign. Just below Scorpio is Tre Beddau, 'the place of the graves', confirming the Scorpionic taste for death.

Virgo the Virgin is located in a triangle of roads below Caio forming a sheaf of wheat. Her body is delineated by the neighbouring hills. Leo is formed from a road leading to Bwlch-y-Maid and the junction of the rivers Gwynau and Cothi. A wood to the west of Leo provides the outline of a boat which is an Earth zodiac sign for Cancer the Crab. Edwards speculated that below Leo once existed a representation of the constellation Hydra, the Water Snake. In Welsh this area is known as 'the back of the serpent'.

Edwards believed that the Welsh star temple was on a stellar alignment which could be found by examining prehistoric tumili on Myndd Llanybydder, south-west of the Earth zodiac. Four cairns are marked on the OS map Edwards used, and they stand in a straight line. He claimed that a line drawn through these monuments and extended into the zodiac circle passes close to the eye of the cosmic bull in Taurus. From this fact he concluded that the Pumpsaint Zodiac had been laid out by astronomer priests in the Age of Taurus, approximately 4,000–2,000 BCE.

Several other alignments were found to bisect the zodiac circle, including one passing through Virgo and a field near Pumpsaint known locally as 'the field of the cross', Maes-y-Groes in Welsh. Edwards believed this was no Christian symbol but a Tau cross used by occult initiates in pagan religions. In the centre of the zodiac he had noted an area by the River Twrch which is surrounded today by the main road to Lampeter and minor roads going to Ffarmers. One of the roads crossed a hillside upon which stood a sacred mound. Edwards identified this as the 'outer sanctuary' used by the zodiac people for public worship. To the south he pinpointed another hill as the site of the 'inner sanctuary' used for secret rituals by the priesthood.

When he was mapping out the Pumpsaint Zodiac, Edwards found an old road which had once been a bridle-path leading north towards Aquarius. This had been a Roman road and was known as Sarn Helen, Helen's Road. St Helen was the Christianized version of Elen, an ancient Celtic goddess who was the patroness of the ley-line system. Edwards also discovered the site of an old burial mound not far away from the Capricorn effigy which was known by the natives as Carreg-y-Bucci, the Goblin Stones. It was said to be haunted and a local farmer who tried to remove stones from the mound was forced to abandon his attempt by a violent thunderstorm. It is claimed that at least three other men had been killed by lightning near the stones.

Two other terrestrial zodiacs are worth mentioning. The first is the Nuthampstead Zodiac located in a part of Hertfordshire frequented by the Knights Templar. As with the Glastonbury, Kingston and Pumpsaint Zodiacs, the earth effigies at Nuthampstead are formed by ancient trackways and earthworks and are confirmed by local place-names and folklore.

In this zodiac Capricorn is the traditional goat, not a unicorn, but the phoenix appears again as the representative of Aquarius. Aries is a ram looking back over its shoulder, as in the insignia of the Templars. The head of the ram is on land owned by a manor which once belonged to a local Templar. After his death fragments of ancient stones were found carved with horned heads. A Roman statue of the god of war, Mars, was also excavated from a local chalk pit.

The Gemini figure has been seen as the Saxon god of winter, death and darkness, called Wandil. He also appears on the Kingston Zodiac in the name of the River Wandle which flows through Merton and Mitcham in Surrey and is, of course, a prominent character in the Gogmagog hill figures at Wandlebury.

Geometrically the Nuthampstead Zodiac is very interesting, for it is criss-crossed with leys and alignments which join together old churches, medieval crosses, prehistoric earthworks, standing stones, moats and ponds. It can be linked with both Wandlebury and Cambridge and is believed by many Earth Mysteries students to have been a pagan centre of sun- and moon-worship.

The second Earth zodiac is at Pendle Hill in Lancashire, which has been a centre for witchcraft practices since the sixteenth century or before. This reputation persists today and is so virulent that a few years ago local Christian evangelists attempted, unsuccessfully, to erect a huge Christian cross on its summit to discourage covens from meeting there. The witches protested at this threat to their religious freedom, and the project was abandoned amid a blaze of sensational publicity.

The Pendle Zodiac is some thirty-two miles in length and allegedly covers a large part of east Lancashire and West Yorkshire. It is therefore claimed to be the largest terrestrial zodiac yet discovered in the British Isles. Robert Lord, who found the zodiac in the 1970s, claims it is of Graeco-Roman origin. He has dated it either from the early centuries of the Roman occupation, *c*. 100–200 CE, or as late as 400 CE, when the Roman legions began to withdraw from Britain. For this reason the symbolism of the Pendle Zodiac is very different from that of the other terrestrial zodiacs so far examined.

For instance, Virgo is a masked and cowled woman and is accompanied by a pet hare – an animal sacred to the moon goddess in both Roman and Celtic mythology. Pisces is a whale swallowing a smaller fish, Sagittarius is a Greek centaur with a bow and arrow, Cancer is the lunar huntress goddess Diana, and Capricorn is the traditional sea goat. Gemini are the twin gods Castor and Pollux of Roman myth, Scorpio is a very traditional scorpion but Aries is a definite ram facing forward with curling horns and has no resemblance to the Templar lamb. Libra is a dove, as in other Earth zodiacs retaining her Venusian influence, Taurus is the bull and Leo a roaring lion. Aquarius appears as a naked male figure whom Lord claims as either Hercules or Bel as examples of the pagan sun god.

The Earth zodiacs are huge figures formed by geographical features in the countryside which may be artificial or natural but other landscape carvings exist which, although on a smaller scale, were no less important to the ancients who followed the Old Religion. These are the labyrinths and mazes which are sometimes called 'Troy towns' in the English folk-tradition.

Most people's conception of mazes is derived from the famous Cretan labyrinth, which was circular in pattern. It is thought to have been introduced into the Mediterranean area around 1600 BCE and to have spread westward. This maze design is found in the British Isles, to which it was supposed to have been brought by the Trojans; hence its popular nickname. However, the earliest known spiral or maze design can be dated back to the Old Stone Age and was found in a

Siberian cave tomb from this period. Many types of the classical maze have been discovered on the floors of Roman villas in Britain. The Roman historian Pliny also describes mazes 'formed in the fields for the entertainment of children', which suggests that his countrymen had lost the original significance of these carvings.

The design of most of the English turf mazes or Troy towns is based on the so-called Chartres spiral, from the famous example in the medieval French cathedral. This maze form predates the Middle Ages, and both Greek and Roman examples have been found. Earth Mysteries writer Nigel Pennick believes this maze design should be termed 'Christianized' because of its widespread popularity in medieval churches and cathedrals.

In the Middle Ages mazes became an essential aspect of the Christian religion. The Chartres maze dates from the thirteenth century and is carved into the flagstone of the cathedral's nave. It is based on a fourfold symmetry and is centred on a non-Christian equal-armed cross. Unlike the more complex Cretan version, it has only one path, which, instead of following a spiral route around the labyrinth, leads directly to the centre. The Chartres maze can still be 'danced' in the pagan fashion, preferably without shoes so that direct contact is made with the earth by the bare feet, albeit through the stones of the cathedral floor. It has been suggested that the maze at Chartres was a Templar innovation, as they are reputed to have been associated with the building of the cathedral.

It is difficult to tell when the English turf mazes were constructed. They may be of pagan date or merely copies of Christianized mazes of the Middle Ages. Mazes were certainly associated with pagan beliefs, for in the seventeenth century, when the Puritans were busy banning pagan festivals such as Christmas (the winter solstice) and May Day, the use of turf mazes for country dancing was also prohibited. The Puritans speeded up the process of neglect, which had been noted by Shakespeare, who said, 'The quaint mazes on the wanton

green are, for lack of tread, undistinguishable.' With the
Restoration in 1660 and the crowning of the 'Merry Monarch',
Charles II, some of the mazes were restored, but only a few
survive today.

In the Middle Ages the mazes were a focus of the May Day
celebrations, and maypoles were erected close to them. It is said
that monks used to go around the mazes on their knees as a
penance if they had sinned. Judging from the pagan beliefs
which were practised near mazes, it would seem that more sins
were committed than were ever forgiven in their vicinity!
Interestingly, Christians called the mazes 'Jerusalems',
believing they represented the sacred city described in the Book
of Revelations.

Several examples of the ancient Cretan labyrinth survive in
the British Isles, and each one is called Troy Town or the City of
Troy, indicating their alleged classical origin. One example can
be found near Delby in Yorkshire, where the original maze was
destroyed in the nineteenth century but restored in the 1930s
and is now protected by the local council. Another Troy Town
exists at St Agnes on the Scilly Isles and dates from the sixth
century CE. Local opinion has it that the maze was carved by
Irish monks who belonged to the Celtic Church. However, its
pagan design indicates an earlier origin.

Another Troy Town exists at the aptly named Troy Farm
near Somerton (?) in Oxfordshire. It is said this maze is a
medieval Christian one, as it is similar to one in a French abbey
dating from the thirteenth century. Two Cretan-type labyrinths can also be found at Rocky Valley near Arthur's
birthplace at Tintagel, Cornwall. These are connected with the
Celtic monk St Nectan, who lived in a hermit's cell in the valley.
They are carved on a rockface, so may be pre-Christian.

Five other Cretan labyrinths can be found carved on a cliff
face at Rockshaw Quarry near Redhill in Surrey. They have
been dated as late as the early eighteenth century and may have
been drawn by workers from the quarry. Presumably they
copied ancient designs. Stone from this site was used to build
Westminster Abbey in the fourteenth century.

The most famous, if controversial, maze is the largest and allegedly surrounds Glastonbury Tor. It is of Cretan design and consists of seven paths carved from the ridges on the side of the hill. The concept of the tor maze was first put forward by Geoffrey Russell in the late 1960s and was expanded by the Arthurian writer Geoffrey Ashe in 1979.

There are two routes taken by the maze paths from the base of the tor. The first route can be traced from the Well House Lane approach to the tor, while the second begins on the opposite side of the hill. Both end at the tower of the ruined chapel of St Michael on the summit, which was the site of a stone circle long since vanished.

The purpose of the maze, like so many things about modern Glastonbury, is a matter for speculation and myth. Geoffrey Russell compared the maze to the Celtic Caer Sidi, the 'turning' or spiral castle which was the home of the star goddess Arianrhod. This Otherworldly place was also said to be the location of Ceridwen's cauldron of inspiration, which in Christian myth became the Holy Grail. Geoffrey Ashe postulates a neolithic origin for the maze and connects it with the worship of the Goddess at Glastonbury in ancient times. He regards the tor as the British version of the 'holy mountain' found in many religions. Both writers agree that the maze was walked or danced for ritual purposes and was used for initiations.

This idea of mazes and labyrinths as initiatory centres is one which is widely accepted in the literature on the subject. The initiate walks or dances the maze and encounters a half-human, half-beast creature at its centre. This hybrid creation represents the initiate's lower self which has to be symbolically fought and subdued in order for initiation into the mysteries to be granted. In some esoteric traditions the object found at the centre of the maze is a mirror which reflects back the initiate's image.

In the Scandinavian and English mazes a game was played in which a young boy finds a maiden representing a princess at the centre. This folk-ritual may be a survival of a pagan ritual which involved a human hero fighting a god of darkness who is holding captive the sun goddess at the centre of the labyrinth. This motif appears in the legend of Theseus, who saves Ariadne from the clutches of the Minotaur, and also features in traditional fairy tales of knights saving maidens from dragons or other monsters.

Many of the Scandinavian mazes are found in groves which were used for the worship of the Earth goddess Nerthus and the sky god Ull. In spring these mazes were the places where the 'sacred marriage' between the god and the goddess were re-enacted by a priest and priestess. Several of the northern mazes are situated in burial grounds, and there is an old tradition that the maze could be used as an entrance to the underworld. In the British Isles mazes can be found carved on the ancient stone at the Bryn-Celli-Ddu burial chamber on Angelsey, North Wales, and in Ireland on the stones at the entrance to the burial mound of Newgrange. As seen in Chapter 3, prehistoric burial chambers may have been used for initiation ceremonies as well as for the disposal of the dead.

6

HOLY WELLS
AND
SACRED SPRINGS

When Alfred Watkins was researching the ley-line system in rural Herefordshire during the 1920s, he paid particular attention to the holy wells and sacred springs which he found on the alignments. In *The Old Straight Track* he says, 'Repeated evidence in ley hunting show tracks straight for them' (holy wells). He also mentions a fellow-researcher who discovered a ley following a track through an orchard which ended at a holy well called Coldwell or, as Watkins interpreted the name, Cole Well.

In the same passage Watkins draws attention to the fact that churches were often built either over or alongside holy wells of pagan origin and that some churches had wells in their graveyards. Winchester Cathedral has a spring under its high altar, and the bubbling springs in the grounds of Wells Cathedral are famous. It is obvious that in pre-Christian times holy wells and sacred springs were part of pagan religious complexes which in many cases became the site of churches as the new religion took over from the old ways of worship.

Today, in our modern era of piped water which flows directly into homes, it is difficult to realize how important wells and springs were to our ancestors. This importance was reflected in the way these sites were seen as sacred places and the centre for religious practices. There is archaeological evidence for pre-Celtic water worship and the Celts adopted many of the beliefs of the indigenous people, which included the reverence of sacred springs and their attendant water deities.

The Celtic worship of wells, springs, rivers and streams was based on the feminine aspect of divinity, and specifically the Mother Goddess. The Celts associated wells and springs with the Goddess because they bubbled up from underground sources. In both Celtic and pre-Celtic belief, caves and grottoes were symbolic of the underworld and the womb of the Great Mother. The entrance to a cave or cleft in the earth from which springs came was recognized as the vagina of the Goddess. In pagan times such places were the scene of divinatory rites and oracular prophecies, and places where the sick could be healed by exposure to the feminine energy flowing out of the earth. Underground caves and grottoes were also used for initiation ceremonies by the ancients, including the Celts and the founders of the classical mysteries.

Rivers were also named after the Goddess by the Celts who regarded water as a sacred substance possessing spiritual qualities and healing power. In ancient Gaul (France) the River Marne took its name from the Celtic deity Matrona, the Divine Mother. The River Seine flowing through Paris received its name from the goddess Sequana, while in Ireland the River Boyne was named after the Celtic deity Boann. In the Irish myths the water goddess mates with Dagda, the phallic fertility god, whom some experts have identified with the Cerne Abbas giant. Dagda owned a cauldron which had the power to revive the dead. This sacred vessel may have been borrowed from an earlier Mother Goddess as patriarchy replaced the older, matrifocal cults of the feminine principle.

In Britain the Celtic tradition of naming rivers after popular tribal goddesses was also practised. Here we can find the River Dee named after Deva, the Severn in Gloucestershire named after the goddess Sabrina, the River Thames called after Tamiesis or Isis, and the Brent in Middlesex named after the goddess Brigantia. In Wales the Welsh word for river, Afon, is believed to derive from the name of a Celtic war goddess, Arfen; in Scotland the Clyde was named for the goddess Clota.

Of these ancient rivers the most interesting is the Severn, where the worship of the Celtic goddess Sabrina is also associated with the water god Nodens or Nudd, who was a patron of healing. His son was Gwyn, who was the leader of the Wild Hunt at Glastonbury Tor. A shrine dedicated to Noden was recently excavated in the region of the Severn estuary at Lydney in Gloucestershire. Noden is linked with the Irish god Nuadda of the Silver Arm, who was a super-hero of the mythical Tuatha dé Danaan, the People of the Mother Goddess Danu who colonized ancient Ireland. The sanctuary dedicated to Nodens at Lydney was a large building which included a hostel for pilgrims visiting the shrine for worship or healing. It dates from the Romano-British period, *c.* third century CE, but was built on the site of an earlier shrine of the Celtic god of pre-Roman origin.

At Lydney, Nodens was equated by the Romans with their solar god of healing, Apollo. The Celts also knew of Apollo and called him Cunomaglus, 'the Lord of the Hounds', which provides a link between Nodens, Gwyn and the legend of the Wild Hunt. Nodens is also associated at Lydney with the Roman god of the woods, Silvanus, who, along with the Celtic stag god Cernnunos, became the role model for the medieval Green Men foliate masks found in old churches built on pagan sites. Nodens was the consort of a Mother Goddess holding a cornucopia whose image was also discovered at Lydney.

It is from Celtic religious beliefs that many of the surviving folk-customs connected with holy wells are derived. Although the Celts were a sophisticated race, like most ancient people they also had barbaric traits, including the unpleasant practice of head-hunting. It was a Celtic custom to decapitate an enemy and display the skull as a war trophy. Over the centuries many religious beliefs became associated with this grisly practice of collecting human heads. Some of these beliefs also became linked with holy wells which were used for healing purposes. There are several recorded instances where a sick person visiting a well had to drink the healing waters out of a human skull.

In some cases these skulls belonged to local nobles or saints. The best-known example of the Celtic head cult in historical times is the legend of St Winifrede, a Celtic saint who lived in North Wales during the eighth century. She was the virgin daughter of a Welsh chieftain who became the object of the sexual advances of the Welsh prince Caradoc. Winifrede fled from the prince and sought sanctuary in a church. Caradoc pursued her, and when she again rejected his overtures outside the church, he cut off her head with his sword.

The spot on the ground where Winifrede's head fell immediately began to gush pure water, to the astonishment of the Welsh prince, who stood open-mouthed at the miraculous sight. At that instant Winifrede's uncle, St Beuno, came out of the church and, seeing what had happened, cursed Caradoc, who fell dead. Beuno replaced his niece's severed head on her neck and breathed into her nostrils, and immediately the wound was healed and she became alive. The place where the spring burst from the ground was named Holy Well, and from the Middle Ages down to modern days it has been regarded as a healing site by Christian pilgrims.

It is unlikely that St Winifrede's well actually dates only from the eighth century. The legend, with its pagan overtones of illicit sexuality, severed heads, miraculous flowing waters, curses, death, rebirth and healing indicates that the area may have been the pre-Christian site of a well or spring used for religious ceremonies.

The cult of the water deities became highly developed when the Romans took over many of the Celtic practices. A local water goddess called Arnemetia was worshipped in Derbyshire at the site of the modern town of Buxton, renowned for its mineral waters and as a spa. The Romans called Buxton *Aquae Arnemetia*, 'the waters of the goddess Arnemetia'. This site was the centre of a Romano-British religious cult involving the curing of diseases by immersing the patient in the healing waters of the spring.

One of the important archaeological finds dating from that period of Romano-British water-worship is the discovery of a well dedicated to the goddess Coventina in Northumberland (Cumbria). Her temple was in the form of a square and enclosed a well originating from an underground spring. This well was very ancient and was originally known as 'the Well of the Nymphs'. This dedication to the nymphs, the elemental spirits of water, suggests a pre-Celtic origin.

Coventina was a healing goddess whose powers were invoked by women seeking cures for menstruation problems, sexual difficulties and the after-affects of childbirth. Her devotees threw small items of jewellery, coins or pins into the pool by the well as votive offerings to the goddess. Other offerings found in the well included small bronze figurines of a horse and a dog, which were animals sacred to the goddess, pottery, small bells and a human skull which is an obvious relic of Celtic head-worship.

The well was the central temple of a localized cultus of water-worship embracing three other shrines dedicated to local water nymphs. A plaque has been found at the main site depicting Coventina as the triple goddess worshipped by the Celts who was sometimes called 'the Three Mothers'. Several other female figures have been located in the area representing water goddesses. One of these is dedicated in Latin to the '*Nymphis et genio loci*' – 'the nymph of the place', who is an early version of the goddess.

The most famous sacred spring in Britain which can be traced back to Celtic times, and before, is the one in Bath. Today it is referred to as 'the Roman baths' but in fact the site includes a pre-Roman temple enclosure and a sacred spring which is older than both. As with the later Christianization of pagan sites, the Romans took over many of the pre-Celtic and

Celtic sacred places for their own worship. The Romans recognized the Celtic gods as the native equivalents of their classical pantheon, and they respected the indigenous forms of worship. In fact, the Roman legions moved against the Druids only to destroy their political power, not to exterminate the Celtic religion *per se*.

Before the Romans occupied the Bath area, the sacred spring had been a centre for the worship of the Celtic water goddess Sul or Sulis. She was accepted by the Romans as a version of Minerva, a virgin goddess who was patroness of mathematics and musical instruments, musicians, craftsmen, artists and warriors. Minerva was of Etruscan origin and has been compared with the Greek goddess Athene.

In the Celtic language the word *sulis* means 'an orifice', 'gap' or 'eye'. This could refer to the symbolism of clefts in rocks as the vagina of the goddess, for at Bath the springs are forced up through cracks in the earth. The different aspects of Sulis Minerva have suggested to Earth Mysteries writer Bob Stewart, who has investigated the site in depth, that she was a version of the Celtic triple goddess. She is identified with the changing phases of the moon and appears as a virgin (new moon), mother (full) and old crone (waning or dark). Some evidence of this was provided at Bath by the discovery of an inscription dedicating the springs to the Roman moon goddess Diana. This goddess was the Roman equivalent of the Greek deity Artemis, who was a virgin huntress, a goddess of fertility represented with numerous breasts, the mistress of beasts and the Lady of All Wild Things. At Bath the goddess Diana is symbolized as a lunar deity with her long hair tied up in a shell and carrying a whip.

Stewart identified the goddess of the springs at Bath as an ancient, possibly pre-Celtic deity of the moon and the underworld. He suggests that her worship involved oracles, divination and initiation into secret rites which required a knowledge of the Otherworld. He believes Sulis was associated with a sun god who was also worshipped locally and might be the Celtic deity Bel or Belinus, known to the Romans as Apollo. His image, misidentified as a gorgon, can be seen at the Roman baths.

The Goddess or feminine principle was divided into so many different aspects in pagan religion that it is sometimes difficult to discover which of them were associated with holy wells, sacred springs and water worship. From the available evidence, it can be surmised that it was usually the Great Mother aspect, who could be either a lunar or earth goddess, depending upon the circumstances of her worship. Epona, the Celtic horse goddess who appears carved in the English countryside at Uffington, has also been identified with holy wells. Her symbol of the cornucopia can be found at Noden's shrine on the Severn, and her function as a goddess who suckles a foal links her with the nourishing and healing powers of the sacred springs. She is also, of course, a goddess of the moon.

Other aspects of the Goddess which were invoked at wells specifically for the treatment of so-called 'women's troubles' are represented in Celtic iconography as nubile, naked young women. These representations have been dubbed 'Celtic Venuses' by archaeologists. However, as these figures often display solar imagery, it is possible they pre-date the patriarchal period and are survivals of the worship of a primeval sun goddess.

With the arrival of Christianity in Britain, the pagan cult of the holy well or spring was transformed. Those Romans who had already been converted to the new faith and the Celts who belonged to the Celtic Church were largely sympathetic to the old ways, and at first the two religions co-existed. The Saxon mercenaries, who had been invited by the Romans to Britain to keep law and order as the legions retreated back to Rome, where pagans who introduced the worship of the Germanic-Nordic pantheon. This included the shaman god Woden, the thunder god Thor, the warrior god Tiw and the earth goddess Nerthus. When St Augustine arrived in Kent with his missionaries at the end of the sixth century, the old pagan sites were taken over for Christian worship. This did not, however, totally eradicate paganism, and in the eighth century bishops were forced to outlaw pagan practices, including the lighting of sacred fires, the worship of trees and stones, and the veneration of holy wells and sacred springs. As late as the eleventh century, King Canute had to prohibit the practice of paganism which involved worship at holy wells.

As with the other pagan sacred places, the Church took over the wells and springs and converted them to Christian worship. The water shrines became centres for Christian baptism, and devotional chapels were built either over wells to incorporate them into the building or in their close vicinity. Many of the sacred springs where the worship of the Goddess was a feature were re-dedicated to the Virgin Mary. The Church had realized that the masses would not give up their love of the feminine principle. Therefore the mother of Jesus was elevated to divine status, and the Marian cultus was developed, encouraged by the Templars and other heretical groups who respected the feminine.

In Britain there are over 150 wells dedicated to the Virgin Mary, and in Ireland many more are dedicated to St Bridget or Bride, the Christianized version of the pagan goddess Brighde who was the patroness of the sacred fires, smithcraft, poetry, childbirth and holy wells. Brighde was a solar goddess whose name means 'the Bright One'. She was allegedly one of three sisters a daughter of the Irish god Dagda and was associated with the Three Mothers or triple goddess of Celtic myth. Her festival was Imbolc (2 February) named from the Celtic for 'ewe's milk', which refers to the traditional start of the lambing season. In Christian mythology, Brighde or Bridget was the midwife of Mary and became wet-nurse to Jesus.

Evidence of early pagan worship at wells can be found in the existence of megalithic remains near their sites. Often these pre-Christian stones were used as natural chairs on which the pilgrims sat either to rest after their journey or to receive healing from the waters administered by the local priest or the person chosen to be the guardian of the well. Many of these stones were carved with Christian crosses to render their pagan powers impotent, but often, it seems, this precaution was not successful. There are many cases of stones near holy wells being used in magical rites to curse an enemy. Sometimes, in a throwback to their pagan use, they were used to swear oaths or make promises that could not be broken, on fear of death.

At St David's in Pembrokeshire, West Wales, there is evidence of a holy well dating back to pagan times which was taken over by the Celtic Church. This well is dedicated to St Non or Nonna, the mother of the patron saint of Wales, St David. According to legend, St Non was a pagan and David was conceived as a result of her rape by King Sanctus of Ceredigion. David was born during a thunderstorm while St Non was sheltering in a cromlech, a neolithic burial chamber.

St Non's well is situated about a mile south of the medieval cathedral of St David's, overlooking the sea and near the remains of a stone circle. Next to it are the ruins of an early chapel whose dedication is to St Non. This chapel is not orientated in the usual Christian manner but north–south, like a pagan temple. The place was in use until the Reformation and was an important centre for pilgrimage.

During the Middle Ages the well became the site for healing rituals and was specifically used to cure eye diseases. Mothers also visited the shrine to immerse their babies in the well to ensure they had a long and healthy life. It also gained a reputation among the local populace as a wishing-well into which coins were tossed. The well was restored by the Roman Church in 1951, when a statue of St Non was erected. It is still visited by pilgrims, pagan and Christian, seeking cures, and votive offerings of flowers and coins are made to the spirit of the place.

The pagan ceremonies practised at the holy wells were replaced in the Christian period by devotional pilgrimages and also by the folk-custom of well-dressing. Holy wells were visited on special days of the year, often coinciding with the old Celtic fire festivals, and were 'dressed' with flowers. This practice was a Christianized version of the placing of flower garlands at sacred springs to appease the water spirits or the goddess who was worshipped there. Today well-dressing is a sophisticated art form, involving the making of elaborate pictures of religious subjects using thousands of flower petals.

Ancient customs of votive offerings also survived the Christian conversion and featured in later rituals at holy wells. This was a symbolic sacrifice when pins, coins, flowers and items of personal jewellery were thrown into the water as an offering for the nature spirit, goddess or saint who was believed to reside there. Sometimes the afflicted part of a sick person was wiped with a cloth using water from the well. This rag was then hung on a tree near the well, and it was believed that as it rotted away so the patient would recover.

The belief that wells and springs were once sacred to the Goddess survived into historical times in a garbled form in popular folklore. There are many stories of mysterious 'white ladies' and 'women in green' who materialize at holy wells and frighten the peasants. In most cases these ghostly figures are benevolent. Occasionally they have been known to utter prophecies, give good advice or point out the location of buried treasure to those who see them. Holy wells are also the habitat of the Little People, Good Folk or faeries, who in folk-memory are often debased forms of the old pagan gods. The association between local people who were considered hereditary guardians of the wells and these sites is obviously a racial memory of the priests and priestesses who administered them in the days before the coming of Christianity.

The way in which Christianity took over the cult of the holy wells from paganism is exemplified by the spring which lies at the heart of Glastonbury. Chalice Well is supplied by an ancient spring which feeds 25,000 gallons of water every day along a pipeline which passes through the Chalice Garden. Today Chalice Well is administered by a private religious trust, and the modern pilgrim can drink the healing water from a fawcet in the shape of a lion's head in the garden. The first reference to the well dates from the thirteenth century, when it was called Chalcwelle. The main road which borders the site is still known by its medieval name of Chilkwell or Chalkwell Street. When the site received its modern name, Chalice Well, is not known but it must have been in the post-medieval period.

The structure around the actual well is of medieval origin and has been dated to the twelfth century. It has been suggested that the stones used to build the walls of the present well were salvaged from the fire which destroyed the original abbey in 1184. Certainly there are accounts of a water-supply diverted from Chalice Well which was used by the abbey in 1220, but the source of the well in a natural spring is far older than these first medieval references.

Whoever was responsible for constructing the medieval edifice of the well used an unusual design. It consists of two chambers built of massive stones. The inner chamber is pentagon-shaped and is reached by an opening in the first chamber, which forms the well shaft leading down to the original shaft. The structure is orientated north–south, which is a pagan feature.

The odd shape of the well chamber has led to some speculation about its use. The occultist Dion Fortune, who lived for many years in Glastonbury, believed it was built of 'great blocks of stone such as were used at Stonehenge'. She claimed when the sun rose over the tor on Midsummer's Day a ray of sunlight shone into the inner chamber. In one wall of the chamber, she claimed there was a recess in which a man could stand upright. Ignoring the medieval origin of the well chamber, Fortune stated it had been a place of druidic human sacrifice. The fact that the spring feeding the well is rich in iron, causing the water to run red sometimes, has led to speculation by other occult writers that Chalice Well was the scene of pagan sacrifices. Its popular name 'Blood Spring' has added to this myth.

On a more positive level, it is a fact that since early times Chalice Well was the centre of a healing cult. In 1582 the Elizabethan astrologer Dr John Dee claimed he had found the *elixir vitae*, the water of life, at Glastonbury, which sounds like a reference to the healing properties of the well. In the eighteenth century a local man published his account of a dream in which he was told to drink a glass of water from the well every Sunday morning for seven weeks. If he did this, he was told, his asthma would be cured. The man followed the advice and was duly cured. This miraculous event was widely publicised, and in May 1751 over 10,000 people invaded the town, seeking cures at the well. Glastonbury became so popular for its healing waters that in 1752 the Bath Room and Pump House were built to supply the demand from pilgrims for the water. A book filled with testimonials as to the well's curative powers was published, with each statement sworn before a magistrate. According to this document, the well water could cure the palsy (Parkinson's Disease), stomach ulcers, eye disorders and deafness.

In the twelfth century the land on which the well stood was owned by a local family who were hereditary bakers to the abbey. In 1189 the son of the master baker married into the family of the hereditary launderers who also worked for the monks. It has been suggested that water from the healing well was used for the mundane task of washing the brethren's dirty habits.

After the Reformation, when Henry VIII closed the abbey, the ownership of the well is obscure. In the nineteenth century it was owned by a Roman Catholic religious order who allowed pilgrims to enter the garden and drink the water. In 1919 a new wrought-iron cover was attached to the well. Its design, based on a thirteenth-century design, includes the pagan symbol of the *vescis piscia*, representing the feminine principle, pierced by an Arthurian lance. The well cover was consecrated in a special service performed by the archdeacon of Wells Cathedral on All Saints Day (1 November or Samhain) 1919. In 1959 the site was purchased by the Chalice Well Trust, in whose safekeeping this sacred site remains today.

The association of the pagan Goddess with caves and grottoes has previously been explained as one aspect of the popular veneration of the feminine principle in the symbolic form of the womb or vagina. In ancient rituals the role of the Goddess was taken by a priestess who represented her in human form. The body of the priestess was the living altar which was worshipped by the congregation as a symbol of the Goddess incarnate. This act of worship was often carried out in grottoes which were places of initiation into the feminine mysteries.

The most unusual grotto of this kind in the British Isles is in the Kent seaside resort of Margate. It is known as 'the Shell Temple', for reasons which will soon become obvious. The Margate Grotto was discovered by accident in 1835 when a group of schoolboys were digging on some land adjacent to a school in Dane Hill. A spade slipped from one of the boy's hands and fell down what was first thought to be an abandoned well shaft. The children called the headmaster, James Newlove, who lowered his son Joshua on a rope into the aperture, with an oil lamp. When the boy was hauled up, he told a fantastic story about a temple with serpentine passages leading to a central chamber and walls decorated with strange symbols formed from sea shells.

James Newlove immediately recognized the find as both an important archaeological discovery and a possible commercial enterprise. He promptly purchased the land under which the grotto lay and dug a passage some thirty-six feet long and four feet wide into the chalk until he found the entrance to the temple. In 1837 he opened it to the public as a tourist attraction and charged the thousands of people who flocked to see 'the Shell Temple' a small admission fee. Unfortunately the gas lighting he installed to enable the visitors to see the interior walls of the grotto also damaged the shells, which became discoloured.

In traditional pagan style, the grotto is orientated north–south, and it is 104 feet in length. In shape it resembles the megalithic 'serpent' traced by William Stukeley at Avebury in the eighteenth century. It has a coiling passage which leads from the entrance to the rotunda in the centre of the complex. Here the visitor can take either a right or a left turn to reach the dome or middle temple. The dome has an opening to ground-level, which was the entrance discovered by the Victorian schoolboys. From the dome runs another serpentine passage leading to the main rectangular chamber, which measures ten by twenty feet. This is known as 'the altar chamber' and suffered bomb damage during the last war. Plaster now replaces the original panels of shells which once covered its walls from top to bottom.

The shells which cover the walls of the grotto suggest that whoever constructed it had a broad knowledge of ancient religions and mythology. The symbols displayed include the signs of the zodiac, pagan gods and goddesses, the moon, sun discs, phalli, snakes, flowers, abstract designs and an anatomically accurate depiction of the female womb. Until the 1940s the figure of a headless female figure carrying a cup could be seen over the entrance arch. Writers on the grotto over the years have claimed that this represents the Mother Goddess, to whom the place was sacred in ancient times.

Conan and Nellie Shaw, authors of *The Shell Temple in Margate* (published privately in 1954), speculated not only that the shells were traced out in intricate occult patterns but that each one was perfectly aligned. The grotto, they claimed, had been constructed in accordance with mathematical calculations which had an esoteric meaning. They believed that it was a secret 'cave of numbers'.

The Shaws were of the opinion that the grotto was connected in some way with the teachings of Pythagoras, who they said was of Phoenician birth. They alleged that following his death several of the philosopher's close disciples formed a secret society who were master masons. This group consisted of a mixture of Phoenician sun-worshippers and Jewish Cabbalists who travelled to Britain 600 years before the birth of the Christ, where they constructed the Shell Temple based on Pythagorean principles. The Shaws suggested that the temple was sealed up in the first century CE to prevent its occult secrets falling into the hands of the Roman invaders.

It is further claimed that the Pythagorean initiates believed that the Supreme Spirit manifested through the sun as the giver of life. Latent within the sun were the potential forces which, when in contact with the Earth personified as a goddess, produced the polarities of positive and negative, masculine and feminine, active and inactive etc. which create the natural world from cosmic nothingness. According to the Shaws, as the centuries passed, the purity of this original wisdom teaching was corrupted. Different names were given to the Supreme Spirit in its solar form, including Ra, Shiva, Jehovah, Bel, Apollo, Baal and Mithras. Usually this solar god was the consort of the Great Mother Goddess in her myriad forms as Isis, Ishtar, Astarte, Danu and Tanith.

In their booklet the Shaws link the Margate Grotto with the worship of the fertility god and goddess Baal and Astarte, represented symbolically by the phallus and the yoni. If, as the Shaws believed, the grotto-builders were Jewish and Phoenician, they would have been familiar with the underground caves used for religious worship in the Middle Eastern desert. In fact, one of the only references to an ancient edifice resembling the Shell Temple at Margate can be found in Chaldea, where archaeologists have found evidence for the existence of two temples decorated inside with sacred reliefs composed of shells, dating from 3,000 BCE.

In the theory put forward by the Shaws, the Margate Grotto was a symbolic representation of the 'sacred marriage' between the sun and moon personified by a god and goddess. The panels of shell designs illustrate the complexity of the life forms which resulted from the unity of these great cosmic forces. This concept is allegedly confirmed by the sacred geometry of the grotto, which is based on the feminine number five. The Shaws point out that the grotto has five arches, five rising sun symbols at the altar, five oyster shells across the altar headstone, five rows of shells forming the altar base and five star designs bordering the altar arch.

Other spiritually significant numbers found inside the grotto include one, representing the Supreme Spirit; two, signifying the manifestation of the duality; three, the holy

trinity found in all world religions, and four, the elemental
forces of the material world. These numbers occur again and
again in the temple design – in borderlines, flower petals,
connecting chains between symbols, and geometric symbols in
the altar chamber. It has been noted that within the Shell
Temple can be found the holy *tetrachtys* of Pythagoras. This is
a symbol consisting of ten circles forming a pyramid. Ten is,
of course, the number reached when one, two, three and four
are added together.

The entrances to the dome are formed by arches which the
Shaws compare to the Gothic arch featured in medieval
cathedrals. In fact, the Gothic arch was not, as generally
supposed, a medieval conception. The masons were heirs to
the mystical tradition which dated back to the Roman College
of Architects and the builders of Solomon's temple. King
Solomon employed Phoenicians to help construct his temple
and imported Egyptian forms of architecture which included
the so-called 'Gothic arch'.

It was suggested by the Shaws that once the dome was open
to the sky to allow the rays of the sun or the moon to penetrate
down into the heart of the grotto. It was their belief that the
grotto-builders had astronomical knowledge. The astrological
signs which decorate its walls, depicting the progression of the
zodiac, allegedly refer to the Aquarian Age which is due to
dawn in the early twenty-first century.

Although, as we have seen, the Shaws were convinced that
the grotto was pre-Christian, its exact age and purpose have
been a matter of controversy. Many eminent people, including
such bestselling writers as H.G. Wells and Marie Corelli,
visited the grotto when it was opened and expressed the view
that it must be thousands of years old. It was rumoured that
the Newlove family had actually constructed the grotto, while
other gossip said it was an eighteenth-century product of the
craze by aristocratic dilettanti for creating artificial grottoes
and Gothic follies. It seems inconceivable that this was so, as
its rediscovery in the 1830s would surely have jogged a few
local memories about its creation in the previous century.

Likewise the effort needed by the Newloves to excavate the grotto would not have gone unnoticed in the locality.

From its distinctive layout alone, it can safely be deduced that the Margate Grotto was a temple for initiation into the mysteries. It can be easily imagined how a neophyte was led along its serpentine passages to be inducted into the lesser mysteries in the dome, the 'outer temple', before entering the holy of holies, the inner sanctum of the altar room. It is more difficult to imagine the type of mysteries the initiate was inducted into in the Shell Temple. However, the Shaws may be right and it could have been a mystical cult dedicated to the goddess of love and her consort.

Evidence for Goddess-worship in ancient Kent has been found. In the 1950s the excavation of a Romano-British shrine at Springhead revealed a female figurine modelled in white clay who was identified as one of the goddesses known as 'the Celtic Venus'. The shrine dates from the first century CE and, as its name suggests, the worship of the Goddess was connected with a healing spring nearby. At Canterbury, the site chosen by St Augustine as a centre for Roman Christianity, another Celtic goddess was found. She sits on a high-backed chair and is suckling twin infants.

It has been suggested that, in addition to the Celtic Goddess-worship which was prevalent, the Phoenicians who visited Britain to trade in tin also established a trading-post at Thanet. In that period the Isle of Thanet was separated from the rest of Kent by the River Wantsum. It has been thought that 'Thanet' may be a corruption of Tanit or Tanith, an ancient moon goddess worshipped by the Phoenicians.

Grottoes sacred to the Goddess were to be found all over Europe in pagan times. In grottoes of this type a series of rough steps led down through the rock to underground caves where natural springs gushed out of the earth. These mysterious places were sites of healing, initiation, rites of purification, oracles and communion with the spirits of the dead.

One famous example of a natural grotto which may have been

used for oracular purposes in southern England is Wookey Hole in Somerset. This network of caves under the Mendip Hills is the source of the River Axe and was occupied by Stone Age people and the Celts. The bones of woolly mammoths and rhinoceroses dating back to the Ice Age have been discovered in the caves by archaeologists. As we have seen, the eighteenth-century Earth Mysteries researcher John Wood believed that Wookey Hole had been the site of a druidic oracle in ancient times.

Wookey Hole, according to a fifteenth-century legend, was once the home of a notorious witch or wise woman. This old lady terrorized the local populace with her evil spells until they sought help from the abbot of Glastonbury. He sent a monk to the caves who sprinkled the witch with holy water and she was turned into stone. This story sounds like a classic tale of the struggle between Christianity and the pagan Old Religion. Modern visitors to Wookey Hole are shown a strangely shaped stalagmite which looks like an old hag. The tourists are told this is the remains of the medieval witch and her dog familiar.

There would appear to be some basis for the story of a witch living in the cave, although not for her petrification by the exorcist monk from Glastonbury! In 1912 archaeological excavations in the cave revealed the skeleton of a woman. Nearby was a 'crystal ball' made of white rock, a dagger, a weaving comb and the remains of two goats tethered to a stake. How the 'witch' of Wookey Hole met her death is not known but the find suggests the cave was once used by a wise woman who possessed psychic powers.

Another witch with prophetic gifts, who was associated with a well and a natural grotto, was the fifteenth-century seeress Mother Shipton. She seems from her physical description to have been the archetypal hag witch with bulging eyes, a long crooked nose, a hunchback and bandy legs. Her fame was based on her prophecies of the future which gained her a wide reputation outside her native Yorkshire. Copies of her predictions are still in print today and her claim that the world would end in 1999 is often quoted.

Mother Shipton lived for part of her life in a cave near Knaresborough, which was popularly described as 'the sybilline grotto' by writers who recounted her legend. From the entrance to the cave can be seen a holy well described in local folklore as an ancient oracle. It is evident Mother Shipton was carrying on the tradition of the pre-Christian priestesses of the Goddess who used holy wells and caves for oracular purposes.

7

MOUNDS AND PYRAMIDS

A variety of different types of burial mound are concentrated in Western Europe dating from the neolithic to the Bronze Age period. Archaeologists generally classify these mounds as burial places used by the ancients to dispose of the dead. The evidence of skeletal remains and grave goods in these mounds offers support for this conclusion. Despite this, there are also some features of these structures which hint at uses other than the burial of corpses or indicate that this may have been a later use in some cases.

The Newgrange burial chamber in the Boyne Valley in Ireland may be an example of this dual purpose. The valley takes its name from the River Boyne which flows through it. As we saw in the last chapter, the river takes its name from a Celtic goddess who performed a 'sacred marriage' with the god Dagda. Newgrange has attracted the attention of both Earth Mysteries researchers and archaeologists because it is astronomically aligned to the rising of the sun at the winter solstice. On this shortest day of the year a beam of sunlight enters the mound entrance, penetrates along its passage and illuminates the central chamber.

It is only comparatively recently that the solar alignment at Newgrange has been confirmed as a fact but its existence was

163

the subject of myth, legend and folklore for thousands of
years. It is yet another example of the survival of pagan
practice through the debased medium of folklore and its
rediscovery in our modern age. In Irish mythology Newgrange
was the legendary home of the Tuatha Dé Danaan who were
worshipped as gods by the ancient Irish. Newgrange was
either one of the entrances to the Otherworld or the actual
realm of the old gods. The original mythical owner was
married to the goddess Boann but in later times his role was
usurped by the phallic god Dagda. His name means 'the good
god', and he was said to have the attributes of divine wisdom
and all-knowledge. Dagda was both a solar deity and a sky god,
and he passed on ownership of the mound to his son Angus or
Oengus, the god of light who was the offspring of Dagda's
mating with the river goddess. The fact that Oengus was a god
of light takes on more significance when related to the solar
alignment at Newgrange.

In medieval accounts there is a tradition that the high kings
of Tara, the Irish royal capital, were buried at Newgrange.
However, in the myths relating to the megalithic mound it is
not a burial-place but the home of the pagan gods. Tara itself
was astronomically aligned, and there are indications in
ancient manuscripts that the Irish Druids knew of the
existence of the seven classical planets. There are also
references to 'Druid temples' of stone used for astronomical
purposes. As the Druids usually met in sacred groves, these
'temples' may have been megalithic circles which were aligned
to the stars and planets. Such knowledge was not, of course, a
druidic invention but would have been inherited from the
ancient people who inhabited Ireland before the Celts.

Newgrange received its modern name in the Middle Ages,
when the land on which it stood belonged to a farm, or grange,
owned by Christian monks. At the end of the seventeenth
century the mound and its adjoining land were purchased by a
wealthy landowner who used some of its facing-stones for road
and dry wall building. It was his workmen who uncovered the
entrance of the mound and revealed the huge stone carved

with spiral symbols which stood there. They dug further and found the opening to the long passage leading to the central chamber in the bowels of the mound.

The discovery of two skeletons inside this chamber led the landowner to decide that it had been a prehistoric underground tomb, and for many years this was the prevailing belief. It was not until 1750 that Charles Vallancey, an English engineer visiting the area to survey maps for the British Army, theorized that the mound had another purpose. Vallancey was regarded as an eccentric by his fellow Army surveyors, who could not understand his fascination with Celtic mythology and stone circles or his theory that the Celtic language derived from Phoenician. When Vallancey claimed that Newgrange was a 'cave of the sun' or solar temple, his idea was greeted with scorn. When he further suggested that many Irish megalithic monuments had been designed to mark the seasonal cycle of the sun, the lunar phases and the progression of the planet, he was dismissed as a crank.

When Vallancey was investigating Newgrange and other sites in the Boyne Valley, the general opinion among the Irish was that these monuments had been built by the Danes. Vallancey dismissed this idea as a fallacy and instead claimed they were of druidical origin and said the Druids were astronomers who used their observation of the stars to predict the future. He may have been incorrect in believing that the Druids were responsible for Newgrange but he had obviously stumbled on the real use of the burial mound and adjacent megalithic sites in the Boyne valley.

One of the first references to the midwinter phenomena at Newgrange in historical times was given by the nineteenth-century mystic, visionary and poet George Russell whose occult works were written under the *nom de plume* 'A.E.'. Russell was a friend of the famous Irish poet W.B. Yeats, who was a member of the Victorian magical group the Hermetic Order of the Golden Dawn. Both men shared an interest in Celtic mythology and were members of the Theosophical Society, founded to reconcile Western and Eastern spiritual traditions. They were also founders of the Fellowship of the Four Jewels, which began in 1916 as an attempt to combine Irish nationalism with a revival of Celtic paganism. The Fellowship was transferred to the United States in the 1930s and was still in existence in the 1970s.

Russell visited Newgrange several times, and on one of these visits he experienced a vision of the god of light, Oengus. In one of his mystical poems written in 1897, he describes a mound into whose interior shines a ray of light which illuminates sacred hieroglyphs on its walls. There can be no doubt that Russell is describing Newgrange and had either witnessed the midwinter sunrise at the site or been told about it by the locals.

The entrance to Newgrange had become covered by thick undergrowth and rubble during the early nineteenth century but in 1849 a local farmer cleared it away. It is therefore feasible that some local people had found out about the solar alignment and told Russell. This happening was fairly well known at the turn of the century, for in 1909 Sir Norman Lockyer casually refers to the fact that Newgrange was orientated to the sun in his book on Stonehenge. This fact was also noted by the American folklorist W. Evans-Wentz, who visited the Boyne Valley studying the local belief in faeries.

Incredibly it was not until the late 1960s that archaeologists began to take the story seriously and realized that the old folk-stories were a reality. The accurate observation of the event and the various theories about it made headline news in the Irish press in 1980, but it was not until 1983 that the research work of an Irish-American expert on megalithic art, Martin Brennan, revealed to the world the truth about Newgrange and other megalithic sites in the Boyne Valley. His researches proved that Newgrange was not unique and that many other burial chambers in the area also had both solar and lunar alignments.

Brennan further discovered that Newgrange was aligned not only to the midwinter solstice sunrise but also to the midsummer sunset, the equinoctial sunsets, the Celtic festivals of Samhain and Imbolc and important lunar dates. It was a site of great astronomical importance, and it seems totally inconceivable that it could have just been used as a burial place.

The most dramatic alignment at Newgrange is the one at the winter solstice. At dawn the sun's rays as it rises above the horizon enter the chamber. A 'roof box' lintel near the entrance to the mound has been designed to divert a narrow beam of sunlight along the passage and project it into the cross-shaped inner chamber. The beam of light passes across the chamber for approximately twenty minutes. For the next hour, as the sun rises higher in the sky, the ray of light leaves the chamber and slowly passes down the passage towards the entrance. Shortly after sunrise, when the light is at its furthest penetration into the passage, it illuminates a triple spiral pattern on one of the huge stones which form the chamber's walls.

At sunset on the winter solstice a ray of sunlight penetrates another burial mound at Dowth, near Newgrange. Because the passage and chamber of this mound are much smaller than those of Newgrange, the light phenomenon lasts over an hour. Again, the stones inside Dowth are carved with mystical symbols, including diamond or lozenge shapes, triangles and serpentine forms. At another burial mound at Loughcrew it was found that the rising sun on the spring and autumn equinoxes shone on solar symbols carved on the stones inside its cross-shaped chamber.

Brennan's study of the megalithic art forms in the Boyne Valley isolated a definite series of symbols which were of either astronomical or religious significance to the ancients. These symbols included equal-armed crosses, eight-pointed stars, circles, diamonds, lunar crescents, ovoids, zigzag lines, spirals – single and double, solar wheels, triangles – upright and reversed, serpentine forms and wavy lines.

He has identified some of these signs as obviously solar-orientated, while he believes others represent the monthly lunar phases or the moon's cycles during the year. He sees the wavy lines and the crescents as archetypal lunar symbols and identifies a stone at Knowlth, which has a wavy line covering its entire length with crescents below, as a soli-lunar calendar.

Several of the solar sigils at Newgrange and other sites are in the form of circles or rayed discs. Others resemble the medieval astrological sign for the sun of a circle with a dot in its centre. Brennan believes that other megalithic symbols represent the major planets, such as Venus, whose brightness in the night sky would have attracted prehistoric astronomers. The triple symbols are representative of the celestial trinity of the sun, moon and Venus, which was considered very important in religious terms by many ancient cultures. The triangular symbols are explained as the cosmic unity symbolized by the seasonal cycle of the year in the megalithic religion.

It is Brennan's belief that the single and double spirals found in the Boyne Valley complex were used to represent the sun's path across the sky, which forms a double spiral pattern. Alternatively the spiral can be a symbol of eternity and, when associated with mazes, is connected with initiation into hidden mysteries. The double spiral at Newgrange is regarded by Brennan as the key to the cosmology of the megalith-builders. He claims their religious beliefs taught that the cosmic unity separated into two principles symbolized by the sun and the moon. In the imagery of megalithic art, the stars are the multiplicity of the universe which is born from the interaction of the twin principles of male and female, light and darkness, and spirit and matter. This process is mythologically presented in the mating between Dagda and Boann, as we have already seen.

What ritual purpose did Newgrange have in the megalithic religion? In the last chapter it was noted that caves and grottoes were the symbols of the womb of the Great Mother. They were also, as at Newgrange, entrances to the underworld and the realm of the Old Gods. In pagan times caves were the site of initiation rituals of death and rebirth. In the classical mysteries of Greece the neophyte was conducted into a cave where he or she experienced a symbolic death. The initiate was then reborn as an 'enlightened one' who had passed from material darkness into the spiritual light. Such rituals were descended from shamanic initiations where the candidate travelled to the underworld to be taught occult secrets by the ancestral spirits and gods.

Solar gods such as Mithras were born in caves, and this pattern can be seen in the story of the Christ and his resurrection or rebirth from the tomb after three days. Many aspects of paganism were grafted onto early Christianity, and the birthday of Jesus on 25 December coincides with the season of the winter solstice and pagan festivals celebrating the birth of Mithras. In fact, Mithraism was a serious rival to the early church, especially among the Roman legions, who were attracted to the cult of the male solar god.

It seems probable that many of the megalithic burial chambers were used for initiation rites. It can be imagined how the neophyte would have entered the inner chamber on the eve of the winter solstice. He or she would have spent the night inside the mound communing with the ancestral spirits and the Shining Ones or tribal gods. At dawn the sun's rays entered the passage and shone into the inner sanctum, illuminating the spiral symbols and the initiate inside. Symbolically the initiate was reborn from the darkness of the womb of the Great Goddess by the rays of the sun god.

The influence of the feminine principle on mounds is exemplified by the example of Silbury Hill in Wiltshire, which is only a few miles from the Avebury complex of stone circles. As with so many of the other ancient places described in this book, Silbury has a potent folk-tradition and has been the focus of extensive research by both Earth Mysteries students and orthodox archaeologists.

Silbury Hill has been described as the largest artificial mound in Europe. It stands at the side of the main A4 road to Bath and is approximately six miles from Marlborough. The mound is in the form of a giant flat-topped cone whose base covers an area of over five acres. Its height is around 130 feet, and it is made up of 12 million cubic feet of earth. It has been calculated that the entire population of modern Britain would need each to bring a bucket of earth to create an identical mound of the same size alongside it. This equation gives some idea of the amount of energy and organization required to build this monument in prehistoric times.

The sides of the mound have an elevation of 30 degrees or 1:2, and near the summit its smooth sides are interrupted by a step or shelf. It has been suggested that the mound was constructed as a stepped cone, which draws parallels with the pyramids of Ancient Egypt and Central America and the ziggurats of Babylon. The reason why the steps are difficult to see today is explained by weathering, although some evidence for their existence can still be found on the side of the mound furthest from the road. It is estimated that when the mound was built it was a third larger than it is today, and has lost some volume through natural erosion.

The name Silbury has been used to describe the mound since at least the thirteenth century. The second part of the name – 'bury' – is of Saxon origin and is often found in connection with earthworks, barrows and burial mounds. In Old English *burh* or bury means 'a defended place' and was used to denote Iron Age hill-forts. According to local folk-tradition, Sil was the name of an ancient king who was buried on horseback inside the mound. It was also said that the hill was raised while a posset or bowl of milk was being boiled! An eighteenth-century story suggests the buried king was actually a life-sized replica of a mounted rider carved from gold.

Silbury was mentioned in 1663 by the antiquarian John Aubrey, who gave King Charles II a conducted tour of the Avebury stone circles. The King saw Silbury Hill and, accompanied by Aubrey, the Duke of York and the royal physician Dr Charlton, climbed the mound. Aubrey told Charles the popular story of the buried king and described Silbury as a 'mausoleum'.

William Stukeley also carried out some research work at Silbury and relates that in 1723 a skeleton was unearthed from the mound which many people believed was the ancient king. The owner of the land on which the mound stood had employed some local labourers to plant trees on its summit. They had dug a large hole and uncovered the rotting bones of the male corpse, which crumbled to dust on exposure to the air. They also found an iron knife with a deer-bone handle, some antlers and two 'brass bits of money'. Six weeks after this, an 'iron chain' was excavated further down the hill. It was very rusty and in a poor condition but Stukeley managed to buy it from one of the workmen and restored it with oil, whereupon it was seen to be a bridle. It has been suggested that this object was Roman, Saxon or even Viking in origin. The fact that the bridle and the knife were made of iron and the presence of the coins would indicate that whoever was buried on top of Silbury Hill had nothing to do with its construction.

The discovery of this burial, however, seemed to confirm the legend of King Sil and, having found one part of the puzzle, the search for the royal treasure believed to have been interred with him went on. In 1776 the Duke of Northumberland became interested in Silbury and brought in Cornish tin miners to dig a vertical shaft down into its core. Nothing was found except an old piece of timber. In the 1840s another team of men dug a tunnel three feet wide and six feet high into the base of the mound. They discovered an inner 'mound' of large stones which was eighty feet in diameter and eight feet in height. Sir Flinders Petrie excavated the base of the mound in the 1920s in an attempt to find the entrance to this inner chamber but failed. Just before the Great War he also explored a tunnel made in 1849 but it collapsed in 1915 and was sealed off by the Office of Works, who administered the site, in 1923.

In 1967 a major archaeological excavation was led by Professor Richard Atkinson, who was sponsored by the BBC 2 programme *Chronicle*. He believed that this attempt would finally solve the mystery of Silbury. The actual 'dig' began in the spring of 1968 in a blaze of publicity, and it continued, on and off, until the summer of the following year. Media interest soon faded when nothing was found, and the archaeologists concluded that the only mystery was why so much time and energy had been expended over the centuries trying to prove the truth of an old folk-tale.

It was not until 1976 that a possible explanation for the real mystery at Silbury was made public. In that year a graduate in geographical science and archaeology, Michael Dames, published his controversial results of an investigation into the hill and its surrounding environment. It provided an alternative explanation for Silbury's construction but it was not one that was easily accepted by orthodox archaeologists or historians. For instance, Dames rejected the idea that the mound dated from the Bronze Age. Instead he accepted the date of 2,660 BCE put forward by the BBC-sponsored team, which put it back into the Neolithic Age. The area around Silbury and Avebury had been settled by early agriculturists who belonged to the Windmill Hill culture, taking its name from another local hill. Dames believed that the answer to the Silbury mystery could be found by examining the Goddess religion practised by the neolithic farmers.

It Dames' contention that the central object of worship by these ancient people was the Mother Goddess, who was often represented in prehistoric art as a naked figure squatting to give birth. Stone Age sculptures show the Goddess with huge breasts, a swollen stomach a distended vagina, emphasizing her fertility and childbearing attributes. According to Dames, Silbury Hill was a gigantic representation of the womb of the Goddess in the landscape. The rest of her body, he claimed, was formed by the silt and water which occupies the surrounding quarry, which also dates from prehistoric times. These features of the Goddess image are defined by the quarry lake, the moat and accompanying ditches which are subject to periodic flooding during the year.

In his published work, Dames points out that in the ancient

cultures which revered the feminine principle the temples for
Goddess-worship were often designed to form the body of a
woman or in the form of a womb or the female sexual organs.
He provides as examples the neolithic temples in Malta and
the so-called 'goddess houses' which can be found on the
Scottish isles of Shetland. He points out that in neolithic art
the eye of the Goddess was a prominent feature. In later
cultures eyes were regarded as spiritually important; hence the
heavy make-up used to outline the eyes of Egyptian
priestesses, the painting of magical charms in the shape of eyes
on the prows of fishing boats, and the widespread belief that
the human eye is 'the mirror of the soul'. Dames regards the
Silbury Hill complex as the 'eye' of the Goddess worshipped
by the neolithic farmers, and considers the mound was a
'sacred mountain' in their belief system.

The unusual folk-story that Silbury was raised while a bowl
of milk was being heated is regarded by Dames as a racial
memory of the original purpose of the mound as a symbol of
the Great Mother. In ancient myths the milk from the breasts
of the Goddess was said to enrich the earth and could pass on
divine wisdom to her worshippers. Statues of the fertility
goddess Astarte had hollow breasts whose nipples were
plugged with soft wax. Hot milk was poured into the statue
which melted the wax and allowed the liquid to pour out into
ritual bowls held by her devotees. In the classical mysteries the
ritual drink given to initiates was often carried in special
containers in the shape of the female breast. There is a
medieval story of the Templars seeking out a Marian shrine
where milk flowed from a statue of the Virgin Mary, which
may be connected with this ancient practice of Goddess-
worship.

Within sight of Silbury Hill is the River Kennet, known in
the Middle Ages as the River Cunnit, which may be a relic of
pagan Goddess-worship, according to Dames. Near it is the
Swallowhead spring which was renowned locally for its
healing properties. In the 1870s the vicar of Avebury
threatened to prosecute the local cunning woman or witch who

made potions from herbs gathered at this spot. The waters
apparently had the power to heal only if they were drunk on
the summit of Silbury Hill.

It is the opinion of Dames that the ancient King Sil was
originally a goddess and could have been linked with Sul, who
is found at Bath in connection with the shrine of the
Romano-British deity Sul-Minerva. He claims that the major
festival of the Great Mother at Silbury coincided with the
harvest in August. Silbury was a symbolic representation of
the cycle of the seasons marked by the sacred festivals of the
solstices and equinoxes and the cross-quarter days which were
later observed by the Celts. He has proved that the mound is
astronomically aligned to the sun/moon rise and set on the
solstices and equinoxes. He has also traced other alignments
from Silbury to megalithic sites in the area.

In 1977 Dames followed up his original research with a
detailed explanation of the seasonal cycle followed by the
neolithic people at Silbury. This not only involved the mound
but also extended out into the countryside to encompass the
West Kennet long barrow, Windmill Hill, the Avebury circles
and even Stonehenge.

The rites performed at Avebury involved the harvest which
was celebrated at the end of August. Three months after this
came the cross-quarter day of 1 November, known to the Celts
as Samhain or 'summer's end'. It still survives today in the
folk-customs of Hallowe'en, when witches, ghosts and goblins
roam abroad and the future can be predicted for the coming
year. (Samhain was the Celtic New Year.) It is a time when the
triple goddess changes from the Great Mother into her old
crone or hag aspect. Dames associates this event at Silbury
with the West Kennet long barrow which was the focus of the
winter rites practised in honour of the feminine principle in
neolithic times.

Candlemass or Imbolc (2 February), sacred to the goddess
Brighde in Celtic mythology, Dames believes was celebrated
in the sanctuary which leads to the Avebury site. He saw this
festival as a time when torchlight processions were held –

which makes sense, as an alternative name for Imbolc in folk-tradition was 'the Festival of Light', and Brighde was the goddess known as 'the Bright One'. He suggests that the sanctuary was also a scene of springtime rites and suggests further that its circular pattern could link to an ancient maze.

Dames accepts the widely held view that Avebury is a feminine site. It was erected in the late neolithic period, which would make it roughly contemporary with Silbury Hill. The fact that the two monuments are in close proximity supports the idea that they were part of the same ritualistic pattern. Dames points out that the convergence of the local Horslip Brook and the River Winterbourne with the Kennet or Cunnit at the Swallowhead spring forms an inverted triangle in the landscape, which is a universal symbol of the feminine principle. He sees Avebury as the ancient centre of a pagan religion which celebrated the 'sacred marriage' between the cosmic forces represented by the sun and moon as symbols of the God and Goddess.

A few miles from Silbury Hill is another ancient hill with a legend of buried treasure. It is Cley Hill, situated just outside the Wiltshire town of Warminster beside the A362 road and almost directly opposite Longleat, the stately home of the Marquis of Bath. In the 1960s Warminster was at the centre of a spate of UFO sightings. People flocked from all over the country to watch the night skies in the hope of seeing one of these celestial visitors, using local heights such as Cley Hill as vantage-points.

Cley Hill has a Bronze Age burial mound on its summit, and prehistoric earthworks which in the Iron Age were the site of a Celtic hill-fort. In local folklore it is said to be the home of the King of the Faeries. In 1588 Cley Hill was one of the beacon points used to warn of the arrival of the Spanish Armada. As late as the nineteenth century, fires were lit on the hill 'to drive away the Devil', and it has been suggested that this was a relic of the ancient sacred fires of pre-Christian paganism.

A legend claims that Cley Hill has a mysterious treasure buried within it. In 1966 a local newspaper reporter, Arthur

Shuttlewood, wrote an article about an inn called the Royal Oak in the village of Crosley near Warminster. This inn was built on the site of a medieval monastery and is reputed to be haunted by the ghost of a hooded monk. The article described how the inn was supposed to be linked to a nearby farm at Winterbourne and Cley Hill by a series of underground passages. Several weeks after the article was published, a mysterious stranger dressed in black visited the inn and requested permission from the landlord to enter the cellars to find the entrance to the tunnels. The publican refused and asked the stranger why he wanted to explore the passages. The reply came that he wanted to locate a magical talisman called 'the golden ram of Satan' which he believed had been buried under Cley Hill many centuries before.

Doreen Valiente, a student of folklore and Earth Mysteries, visited the area and met a local dowser who confirmed that there were tunnels under Cley Hill. She also discovered that the nearby hamlet of Temple gained its name because it was once owned by the Knights Templar. In an article published in the occult magazine *Prediction* some years ago, Valiente speculated that the 'golden ram' may have been an effigy of the Templar deity, Baphomet. The order could have buried it at Cley Hill for safekeeping when the knights were persecuted in the fourteenth century.

Another mysterious mound which seems to have connections with Earth energy and the pagan Old Religion is the so-called Priory Mount in the Sussex town of Lewes. Its name is taken from its close proximity to the remains of the medieval priory of St Pancras, and local folklore claims it was built as a replica of Calvary. The mound is next to a square enclosure called the Dripping Pan. This name has been seen by folklorists as a reference to the drying of fish using salt, which was once a common trade along the south coast. It is alleged that the mound was, in some unknown way, connected with this industry.

Priory Mount is conical in shape and is approximately forty-two feet high. Its top is truncated, with a circular flat apex about twenty feet in diameter. Around the circular base the mound measures approximately 165 feet. It is made of chalk and has the unusual feature of a spiral path which winds up the hillock from the north–west to the top. Part of the mound has been removed to make way for the modern bowling-green which lies at its base.

The age of the mound is difficult to estimate. It is shown on maps of the area dating from the eighteenth century, and archaeologists have suggested it may be of medieval origin, dating back to Norman times. Lewes Castle was built on a hill directly behind it, and there is speculation that Priory Mount may have been raised as an artificial earthwork to support a small fortification or watchtower connected with the main castle. Its religious overtones, as Calvary Mount, obviously link it with the nearby priory. However, the mound is situated outside what were the old priory grounds, and there is no extant tradition of medieval monks constructing such replicas of Calvary elsewhere.

If Priory Mount is not medieval in origin, some writers have suggested it may date back to even earlier times. Earth Mysteries researcher Rodney Castleden has said that he believes the mound was a neolithic 'harvest hill', in the tradition of Silbury Hill, linked with the Long Man of Wilmington a few miles away. Although the mound has never been subjected to an archaeological examination, he points out that the shoulder bone of a cow or ox was found buried in it near the surface. Castleden claims that this might have been a tool used by the neolithic workers responsible for raising the earth structure.

The spiral path leading to the summit of Priory Mount is also significant, and we have seen its importance at Glastonbury, another 'holy hill' or 'sacred mountain' in the English landscape. In ancient belief the spiral represented the path to initiation, the sun's journey through the sky which marked the seasonal cycle of pagan festivals in the ritual year and the journey of self-discovery or the spiritual quest which lies at the centre of all genuine religious and esoteric belief systems.

As Castleden points out, the site of the mount is at present hemmed in by the 'modern' town, and it is difficult to imagine how it must have looked *in situ* at the period when it was originally constructed. The mound is only a few hundred feet from the estuary of the River Ouse and would have been a prominent feature in the flat countryside before the town was built. As we know from Silbury Hill the sacred mound was a very important feature in ancient Goddess-worship. The discovery in early 1989 of the remains of a prehistoric ceremonial structure made of oak posts straddling the River Kennet at Avebury, which supports Michael Dames theories about the site, emphasizes this point. Many of the megalithic sites were deliberately sighted near running water or springs or over underground streams, indicating that water was regarded as an important sacred element by our ancestors.

Priory Mount is situated on raised ground which projects towards the River Ouse. This elevation is crossed by two modern roads which Castleden says were originally a prehistoric trackway. This eventually, he claims, meets up with a neolithic causeway about six miles away and is connected with the famous South Downs Way, an important pre-Roman 'green road' linking several major sacred sites in Sussex.

If the mount is really of prehistoric origin, what was its religious function? According to Castleden, it may have been an ancient solar observatory. This theory fits in with its possible use by the neolithic farmers as a harvest hill in the Silbury Hill model, used to calculate the sacred dates of the year based on the solstices and the equinoxes. Castleden alleges that solar alignments can be traced from the mound to several other hills and Bronze Age barrows surviving in the district. These alignments include the midsummer and midwinter sunrise and sunset used by the neolithic and Bronze Age peoples as seasonal markers for religious and agricultural purposes in their celebration of the natural cycle of the seasons.

Compared with Silbury, Cley Hill and Priory Mount, the pyramids of Ancient Egypt are a sophisticated form of sacred mound building. The earliest examples of pyramids were constructed at the beginning of the Third Dynasty, *c.* 3,000 BCE, in the reign of King Zoser, and were very crude in comparison with later designs. The early pyramids were derived from the pre-dynastic Mastaba tombs. These were rectangular-shaped tombs consisting of an underground burial chamber surmounted by a superstructure which rose up in a diminishing series of steps. Originally the burial chamber inside the tomb was approached from an entrance at the top, but in later examples a passageway descended at right angles from the north to gain access.

Despite their structural crudity, these early pyramids from the reign of Zoser were still impressive and consisted of over 20 million tons of limestone. As the centuries passed, the technique of pyramid-building became more and more sophisticated and peaked with the construction of the Great Pyramid of Giza in 2400 BCE, which stands today as a monument to the skills of the Ancient Egyptian masons.

The Great Pyramid is located ten miles west of Cairo on the plain of Giza. Its height is over 400 feet, and its base covers thirteen acres. It is estimated that over 2 million blocks of granite and limestone, each weighing seventy tons at most, were used to construct the pyramid. Initially the structure was coated with a polished surface of limestone which provided a mirror-like surface. After a series of major earthquakes which devastated Egypt in the Middle Ages, this covering was removed and used to rebuild the damaged houses of Cairo.

Rumours of buried treasure inside the pyramids encouraged grave-robbers, who vandalized the outside walls in an attempt to gain entrance. As early as the seventh century CE an Arab historian wrote that the Great Pyramid contained a huge precious stone carved into the life-size form of a long-dead king. Shades of Silbury Hill! In 820 the caliph of Egypt, Abdullah Al-Mamum, led an expedition to unearth the alleged treasure. His team attempted to smash their way through the pyramid walls using hammers and chisels but they made no impact on the surface. It was decided to heat the stone until it was red hot and then pour cold vinegar onto it to crack the surface. By using this technique the Arab workmen managed to penetrate a hundred feet into the pyramid and eventually found the old entrance and a passageway leading to a large room they called 'the Queen's Chamber'. Eventually they discovered a second room above it, which they called 'the King's Chamber'. Inside this room was an empty sarcophagus made from dark brown granite.

The medieval earthquake had sealed the entrance to the Great Pyramid for several centuries. With a lack of genuine information about its origins, folklore and superstition provided a pseudo-history. Local tales recounted how the place was haunted by dead pharaohs and evil spirits. A twelfth-century rabbi visited Egypt from Navarre and claimed that the pyramid had been erected by witchcraft. This statement was taken up by nineteenth-century occultists who said the Egyptians had levitated the stones into position using magical powers. This is an interesting theory, except that the fifth-century BCE historian Herodotus was told by Egyptian priests that the masons hauled the stones for the pyramids from local quarries. He said the Great Pyramid was built using this unromantic method over a twenty-year period, using 100,000 workers.

In the seventeenth century an English explorer, teacher and astronomer, John Greaves, visited Egypt. He was reliably informed by his Arab guides that the pyramids concealed magical talismans and underground chambers into which the waters of the Nile flowed for ritual purposes. Greaves entered the Great Pyramid in 1639 and was surprised to find that an edifice of this size had, apparently, been built to contain an empty chamber. It is a mystery which has baffled archaeologists ever since. During his investigations, Greaves discovered a passage leading down into the centre. This was only three feet wide and ended some sixty feet further on in a small chamber which he nicknamed 'the grotto'. The purpose of this hidden chamber was also to remain a mystery. Greaves made a careful note of the pyramid's dimensions because he was convinced it originally had an astronomical significance.

Greaves' work on the pyramids was not to be followed up for at least 200 years, until Piazzi Smyth, the Astronomer Royal of Scotland, visited the Great Pyramid and began to take measurements. Considerable interest in the pyramids and Ancient Egypt in general had been created following Napoleon's military campaign in the 1800s. Ancient Egyptian artefacts had become a fashionable feature of the 'salon culture' of the late eighteenth and early nineteenth centuries and influenced the occult revival of the period, with its Masonic and Rosicrucian overtones. One of Napoleon's surveyors, François Jonard, had argued that the pyramids were monuments to the Ancient Egyptian science of sacred measurement. He claimed that the Egyptian priests were skilled in astronomy, physics and geography and had incorporated the measurement of the Earth's circumference into the pyramid dimensions.

These ideas had an influence on Piazzi Smyth, who was a student of Sir John Herschel, the discoverer of the planet Uranus, which was at first named after him. In the 1840s Herschel carried out a survey of the Great Pyramid and noted that its four corners were aligned to the cardinal points. An observer looking along the entrance passage could see a changing section of the night sky as the Earth rotated on its axis.

Smyth was inspired by Herschel's idea that the Great Pyramid may have been used as an ancient astronomical observatory. He was, like Herschel, opposed to the new campaign for metrification which was gaining converts in Britain and believed the inch was a sacred measurement. Smyth seized on the theories of a retired publisher, John Taylor, who in 1859 wrote a book revealing that the standard unit of measurement used by the Egyptians was a 'pyramid inch'. This measurement, John Taylor claimed, represented a 500-millionth of the Earth's polar axis, and he linked it with the belief that the British race were one of the lost tribes of Israel. Taylor believed that the sacred art of Egyptian measurement was taught to the Hebrews while they were in slavery and later formed the foundation of British sacred geometry.

In 1864 Smyth visited Egypt and in the atmosphere of the Khufu pyramid discovered a mason's boss which was allegedly one pyramid inch high. This he identified as the standard unit upon which pyramid-building was based, and further stated that the structures had not been originally designed as tombs but were 'houses of initiation' where the priests and members of the pharaohnic caste were inducted into occult mysteries. He even claimed that the measurements of the pyramids were a secret code which, if deciphered, would reveal passages in the Bible as prophecies of the present age. Smyth's astronomical discoveries were taken up by another astronomer, Richard Proctor, who in the 1880s claimed to have found some ancient Roman writings which related that the pyramids had been erected as astronomical observatories by the Egyptian priests.

In the 1930s further research into the sacred architecture of Ancient Egypt, including the great temples of the Nile and the pyramids, was carried out by a French occultist, René Schwaller, who was a member of the Theosophical Society, a student of the hermetic occult tradition and a follower of Pythagorean philosophy. During his researches into alchemy, Schwaller discovered the medieval method of producing the special stained glass used in the rose windows of Chartres. He spent fifteen years living in Egypt and claimed to have revealed the secrets of Ancient Egyptian symmetry which was based on the dimensions of the human body and the Golden Section or Divine Proportion which featured in medieval cathedral-building and Renaissance art. Schwaller concluded that the architecture of the Egyptian temples was designed to represent the human body as a symbolic form of the hermetic axiom 'As above – so below'.

The term 'pyramid' is from the Greek *pyro*, 'fire', and *mid*, meaning 'centre' or 'middle'. The Ancient Egyptian name for the Great Pyramid is *Khuh*, 'the Lights'. This suggests that Smyth's concept of the pyramids as centres for initiation may have had some basis in fact. Indeed, the Egyptian pyramids can be seen as a sophisticated form of the Western European burial mounds used for the same purpose. The initiate, as its name suggests, would have been spiritually transformed by the mysterious energy force which apparently exists within the pyramidal structure.

The fact that the pyramid's unique shape had some unknown influence was (re-)discovered in the 1950s by a French tourist. Entering one of the pyramids, he noticed the corpse of a cat which must have wandered into the structure and then died. The cat's body was completely mummified. When he returned to France, the tourist constructed a scale model of the pyramid of Giza which he orientated north–south and east–west in the same position as the original full-sized version. He placed the body of a dead cat half way up the pyramid in a position comparable to the siting of the King's Chamber. The cat became mummified within a few days.

The tourist, a M. Bovis, wrote a report on his findings which was read by a Czech radio engineer named Karel Drbal. Following in the Frenchman's footsteps, Drbal also constructed a scale model of the Great Pyramid and conducted a series of scientific experiments. He found that perishable items such as food stayed fresh longer if stored inside a pyramid shape. He was astonished to find that razor blades placed inside the pyramid underwent a molecular transform-ation, and blunt ones became sharp again. In 1959 Drbal patented this idea, producing a 'pyramid razor-blade sharpener' which became very popular in his native Czechoslovakia.

It has been suggested by some occultists that the pyramid shape, or tetrahedron, is similar to one of the seven possible forms made by a natural crystal. This particular shape has the property to create molecular changes which regenerate organic matter. It is noted that the Arab treasure-hunters who entered the Great Pyramid in the Middle Ages found the walls of the Queen's Chamber encrusted with crystalline deposits of salt almost half an inch thick. The pyramid is also a refractor for

light, which could produce energy patterns within its
structure.

Pyramid energy has many different effects which have been
scientifically catalogued. Plants and animals exposed to the
energy increase in growth and are healthier; blood pressure in
humans can be normalized if it is too high or low; fresh milk
does not go sour and is preserved for a longer period; skin
grafts heal faster; polluted water is purified; human auras
increase in strength; metals show a noticeable weight-loss, and
water treated in a pyramid for two weeks has significantly less
bacteria than non-treated water.

Attempts to measure accurately the energy fields of the
actual pyramids have produced either negative or contra-
dictory results. In the early 1980s a scientific project was
sponsored by the US Atomic Energy Commission, the
Smithsonian Institute and the University of Cairo to find
secret chambers inside the Great Pyramid. The method
employed involved projecting cosmic rays into the interior. A
cosmic particle device would indicate a loss of energy in the
passage of the rays through a hidden chamber when compared
with their passage through the solid stone of the pyramid.
When the tests were completed, magnetic tapes of the results
were fed into a computer and analysed. It was found that the
energy readings taken on separate days were all different. In
addition, some of the readings did not register at all. One of
the scientists who took part in the project was quoted as
saying, 'It defies all known laws of science and electronics
which is scientifically impossible. Either the geometry of the
pyramid is in substantial error or there is a mystery here which
is beyond explanation. There is some force which defies
science at work in the pyramids.'

Returning to the mystical symbolism of the pyramids in
Egyptian religion, one of the chief exponents of the theory that
the structures were initiation centres was a French writer,
Edouard Schure, who reconstructed the rites of the mysteries
of Isis and Osiris in 1899. Schure described how the neophyte
entered the pyramid after a long period of fasting and

meditation. In the Queen's (or Isis) Chamber the neophyte was shown the twenty-two symbols of the *Book of Thoth*, which became known as the tarot in medieval times, and their esoteric significance was described. The candidate then had to undergo an ordeal by fire and water and was tempted by a scantily clad Nubian slave. (It is presumed a male slave was available if the neophyte was a woman.) If this ordeal was passed, the candidate then took part in the ritual of Osiris. This involved, according to Schure, the reconstruction of the death and rebirth of Osiris at the hands of the dark god Set and the Ancient Egyptian funeral rites. Hence the symbolism of the empty coffin in the King's (or Osiris) Chamber which was used in these rites. The neophyte was then symbolically reborn as an initiate or illuminated one.

The mystery of the pyramids can be seen as an example of the way in which the study of Earth Mysteries reveals the hidden truths concealed within the ancient religious beliefs of our ancestors. In our examination of ley lines, stone circles, hill figures, Earth zodiacs, mazes, holy wells, sacred springs, grottoes, mounds and pyramids, the spiritual significance of these ancient places has been a primary factor.

8

EARTH MAGIC

It is an unfortunate fact that many orthodox archaeologists still persist in the outdated belief that early humankind was primitive, savage and brutish. However, it is also totally wrong to project our own modern wish-fulfilments of utopia back into the past and claim that in prehistory a perfect society or Golden Age existed which represented a paradise on Earth. The truth most ultimately lies between these two extreme views, although it seems that the concept of a Golden Age, a period when humanity lived in harmony with each other and the natural world, is found in the recurring pattern of creation myths belonging to the oldest cultures on Earth. The idea that this era of peaceful co-existence came to a sudden end when humanity 'fell' from grace and was separated from the natural world can also be found in world religious traditions and ancient mythologies.

For a modern person fully to understand the intellectual or spiritual framework or the mythic models employed by the megalithic culture to comprehend the universe is very difficult. Archaeology and orthodox interpretations of history tend to fall back on the explanation that early humankind lived in constant fear of the natural environment. This fear led to the worship of elemental forces which were regarded with awe and reverence as 'dark gods' which had to be propitiated with bloody rites of sacrifice. The scenario of early humans crouching around their campfires listening to the animal noises in the surrounding darkness and interpreting them as the voices of demons is often presented as an accurate depiction of ancient religious awareness. Natural phenomena such as thunder, lightning, earthquakes, tidal waves, gales and volcanoes were allegedly worshipped because the ancients lived in fear of their destructive power.

These simplistic ideas about early religion are based largely on our own feelings of superiority and on the use of the traditional theory of evolution to explain the historical development of spirituality. The use of these criteria suggests that the religious concepts of humankind have evolved from the primitive worship of Nature to our present abstract, monotheistic vision of divinity. It is presumed that, as modern society is more evolved (allegedly) than prehistoric culture, so our present religious forms are also the ultimate in spiritual expression.

This ethnocentric proposition ignores the fact that, while our own society is in many ways more developed than its prehistoric equivalent, it is a matter of debate whether we are any more evolved than the ancient peoples who erected the stone circles. While they had the capacity to kill possibly several hundred enemies in a battle fought with bows and arrows and spears, we now possess the ability to murder millions with nuclear weapons and the potential to destroy the planet. Today we face the consequences of 'civilization' in the threat from urban terrorism, inner-city crime and industrial pollution which were unknown to our ancestors. In this respect who can say who is the most evolved? While today we have the many benefits – together with the attendant problems – of modern technology, it is true to say that the megalithic culture had its 'magical' technology based on Earth Magic which was expressed in the ley system and the use of the sacred power centres.

In their analysis of the religious beliefs of our prehistoric ancestors, archaeologists and historians have regarded their conceptualization of the sacred as a primitive attempt to represent divinity. The ancient belief of pantheism, defined by the *Oxford English Dictionary* as 'the doctrine that God is everything and everything is God', and animism, the attribution of living soul to inanimate objects and natural phenomena, which were the spiritual foundation of megalithic religion, are largely rejected today. Today these beliefs are generally regarded as atavistic relics believed in only by ancient primitive races and their present-day survivors, such as the native Americans, the Australian Aborigines, the South African Bushmen and the South American tribal peoples. Neo-pagan revivals in modern Western culture are treated with suspicion if not derision in academic and scientific circles, where the pantheistic belief is regarded as an atavistic aberration.

Pantheism was rejected as a heresy by the early Christian Church and has played a minimal role in spirituality in the last 2,000 years, although it has survived as an underground tradition in Western religious thought. The Church regarded God as totally separate from his creation, with man having a unique role outside the natural world over which he was given dominion, as stated in Genesis. Both these concepts were alien to the ancient pre-Christian pagan world view, which regarded matter and spirit as one and did not differentiate between the sacred and the profane. The desacralization of Nature, which was a product of Christianity, divorced humankind from the natural world and created the intellectual outlook which is the *raison d'être* for the destruction of the environment and the depletion of the planet's natural resources for material gain.

It is understandable, in some ways, that the early Church fathers reacted against the excesses of paganism in a negative way. In a period when the established pagan religions were in moral decline, the puritanism of the new faith was accepted by many as an alternative path to spiritual salvation. Christianity had its roots in Jewish monotheism, with its belief in a hidden God who could not be represented in physical form, and was influenced by the Gnostic heresy, which rejected the natural world as an evil illusion created by a false god. To the followers of Christianity, the polytheism of the pagans and their representations of the gods were the unacceptable face of religious belief, and they reacted by condemning these practices as 'heretical', 'heathen' and 'devil-worship'.

When the early Christians denounced the pagan worship of trees, stones and holy wells, they did so because monotheism cannot accept a universe populated by many gods. What they did not understand was that the pagans regarded their gods and goddesses as aspects of the creative life force which they believed flowed through the universe. Belief in a Supreme Deity, who is usually a creator god, can be found in the majority of pagan religious systems. In this context the sacred function of the 'idols' worshipped by pagans was to produce a channel through which divine power could be focused. The sacred centres in the landscape were recognized as special places where humanity could contact the cosmic forces, personified by the gods, and the divine power which manifested through the earth. This belief is graphically illustrated in the tradition of the hill figures, which were symbolic representations of the gods carved into the land to enable the worshipper to make contact with the powers these archetypal images symbolized.

Central to the religious beliefs of the megalithic culture, as we have seen, were the veneration of the feminine principle and the belief that the Earth was symbolically a goddess who had to be worshipped if the fertility of the land and the tribe was to be preserved. This worship was prompted not by fear but by the love of the feminine as a creative force and an understanding of the relationship between humanity and the natural world. As we saw at Silbury, the Earth goddess was often associated with the seasonal cycle which culminated at harvest, which was one of the most important festivals of the year in an agrarian culture.

Early agriculturists traced a connection between the land and women as a source of fertility. The significance of the link between the menstrual cycle, the lunar phases and the planting of crops was an essential element in prehistoric religion in the matrifocal period. The Great Mother was depicted as the supreme creative power which sustained both animal and plant life. As religious symbolism became more sophisticated, the Goddess was regarded as having many aspects and could be the deity of the sun, Earth, stars and moon. When she was worshipped in her lunar aspect, the female deity was the Triple Goddess in her three forms, as maiden (new moon), mother (full moon) and crone (dark moon). It was in this form that she was worshipped by the Celts, as we have seen at Bath and other holy wells and sacred water shrines.

Neolithic representations of the Mother Goddess emphasized her sexual characteristics. The breasts, stomach and thighs are a primary focus point in Stone Age effigies of the feminine principle. Sometimes she is represented as pregnant or even in the act of giving birth. Floral symbols and patterns carved on these statues suggest her control over the growth of vegetation and the agricultural cycle.

In the Middle East exist numerous representations of the Goddess dating from the Bronze and Iron Ages which are comparable to neolithic examples. In these representations, the Goddess is depicted naked with prominent breasts and holding plants in her hands. In most cases the breasts and stomach are emphasized, some are clearly pregnant and others hold a small child. In a few of the images the figure holds her breasts, as if displaying them and the virtues of motherhood. These ancient representations of the feminine principle survived in medieval Christian art as the Sheela-na-gigs found in old churches built on pagan sites. These are carvings of female figures with legs splayed, holding open their vaginas. No satisfactory explanation for the siting of such blatant examples of pagan religious images in churches has been put forward by clerical historians, and they are generally presumed to be a medieval relic of pre-Christian Goddess-worship.

The religious vision of the Earth as sacred and of its cultural and spiritual significance as feminine was an important factor in prehistoric society, when Nature was a primary source of ritual and a focus for worship. Oral tradition, direct experience and active participation were the keynotes of religious expression in pre-literate societies. The pattern of the seasons was woven into the fabric of everyday life, providing a basis for religious inspiration, and each person had a unique perception of the natural environment which surrounded them. This perception was not an analytical one but was centred on first-hand experience of the creative flow of elemental forces and natural rhythms which, cocooned in prisons of concrete and metal, we seldom appreciate today.

However, today increased awareness of the damage humanity is inflicting on the ecological system of the planet is gradually bringing this ancient idea of the Earth as sacred back onto the spiritual agenda. In contrast to the religious beliefs of the hunter-gatherer society of prehistory, today this concept is being presented in an ecological context with a more scientific basis for our modern age. The so-called Gaian hypothesis originated with the theories of Dr James Lovelock, an independent scientist who has worked for NASA and the Department of Cybernetics at Reading University and is a Fellow of the Royal Society. In 1979 Lovelock published the results of his ten-year research into the Gaian concept, named after the Greek earth goddess. He believed that the ancient idea that the Earth was a feminine deity may have been based on the scientific fact that the biosphere is not just the sum total of the range of flora and fauna inhabiting the planet but a living, conscious entity which regulates the environment in an intelligent way.

Lovelock's research indicated that life exists on our world not because material conditions happened to be right at some primeval point in time when the first amoeba formed in the oceans of early Earth but because of the intelligent actions of the planetary entity Gaia. He regards the ancient history of humankind as a period when our ancestors co-existed with

Gaia in a state of harmony. Our technological progress over the last few thousand years is a symptom of our separation from Nature and the Earth which is reflected in the adoption of religious beliefs which deny the feminine principle and the natural world. Since the Industrial Revolution and the so-called Age of Reason, this alienation process has accelerated, with science and technology claiming to be able to improve the environment and our quality of life in ways which would have seemed like magic to our ancestors. Unfortunately the horrific by-products of this march of progress can now be seen in the threat posed to the planet's eco-system by industrial pollution, the damage to the ozone layer, the destruction of the tropical rain forests, the problems of radioactive waste and the fate of endangered species.

The Gaian hypothesis sees humanity as an integral part of the self-regulating system operated by the planetary entity. When past cultures lived in harmony with Mother Earth and worshipped her as a goddess, the amount of damage which occurred to the biosphere was minimal. Today, when the idea of the land and the Earth as sacred which was held by the megalithic culture has been rejected, humankind is in danger of disrupting the environment to such an extent that the future of life on this planet hangs in the ecological balance.

Dr Lovelock believes that Gaia can survive anything our industrial society throws at her by adjusting her life systems to neutralize the pollutants. It has even been suggested by some ecologists that eventually Gaia might decide that the human species is a dangerous parasite which must be eliminated to preserve the future of the biosphere. Others, more controversially, even believe that the modern environmental and green movement may itself be the product of Gaian intervention in human affairs. Writing in the late 1970s, the self-sufficiency expert John Seymour stated that he had become convinced that it can only be some kind of spiritual force which drives ordinary people, consciously or uncon- sciously, to march on nuclear power plants, protest about the bloody slaughter of seals and whales and resist the spread of industrial urbanization. Seymour believed that Gaia was using the ecological lobby to turn us away from ways of living which threatened her existence.

What is the answer to the problem of the destruction of the environment? Those who follow the study of Earth Mysteries believe that the restoration of the old knowledge and the ancient wisdom of the megalithic culture in a modern form may represent one way out of the evolutionary cul-de-sac created by modern man. Those researchers who accept Lovelock's hypothesis as a reality have interpreted the ley system with its energy lines criss-crossing the planet and its power centres as the nervous system of Gaia.

The modern rejection of Mother Earth can be seen in the fact that the natural energy which flowed along the leys was often symbolized as a dragon or serpent. In ancient cultures the Goddess was often associated with a snake, and in Minoan art the figure of the female deity standing bare-breasted holding a serpent in each hand was a popular icon. The followers of the Old Religion regarded the snake as an emblem of immortality because of its ability to shed its skin every year, as if reborn. This reptile became a symbol of wisdom and of the initiate who was born from material darkness into spiritual light or enlightenment in the womb of Mother Earth – the caves or burial chambers which were her shrines or 'womb temples'.

This wisdom imparted by the snake was alleged to be of a divine nature and derived directly from the Goddess. In the Delphic oracle in ancient Greece, before it became the patriarchal centre for the worship of the solar god Apollo, the priestesses acted as oracles for the Great Goddess. These prophetesses were known by the title *pythoni* and were alleged to keep snakes which they used as familiar spirits. The priestess who acted as the oracle sat on a three-legged stool over a crack in the earth from which poured fumes (energy) which inspired her prophecies.

The association of the feminine principle with the serpent or snake is found in the Earth Mysteries field, as stated earlier, where the dragon power which flows along the ley lines is characterized as being of a female nature. This invisible energy has been given many different names in occult and religious tradition, including *prana, ch'i, anima mundi, pneuma, ki, vril* and *orgone,* but its existence has been known for thousands of years by those who revered the Goddess and knew the magical secrets of the sacred landscape of our planet.

In Christian times the dragon or the serpent, the symbol of the Earth energy, has been falsely identified as a symbol of evil and the powers of darkness represented by the old pagan gods. This process is understandable, for the gods of the Old Religion often become the devils of the new. The myth of the Garden of Eden, with its Satanic serpent seducing Eve, was used by the early Church to condemn serpent-worship associated with the Great Goddess and to denigrate the role of priestesses in pagan society as the channel for divine power and the initiators of men into the greater mysteries. Stories of St George slaying the dragon, found at the White Horse of Uffington, and the mumming plays associated with the hobby-horse cultus, and the dedication of pagan sites to St Michael, at Glastonbury Tor in Somerset and Penbryn in West Wales, for instance, are examples of the way in which the new faith sought to control and suppress paganism, the Earth energy and the Goddess.

In one way, the fear of the dragon energy by the early Christians was based on something more than pure superstition, misogyny or a distaste for the hedonism of the pagan beliefs. Modern dowsers have proved that, if the dragon energy is tampered with or misdirected, it can have a detrimental effect on the life forms in its vicinity. In such circumstances the Earth energy can become a manifestation of the Dark Goddess of death and the underworld. The existence of these negative leys was known to the ancients. Plutarch, writing in the first century CE, stated, 'Men are affected by streams of varying potency issuing from the earth. Some of these drive people crazy or cause death or disease; the effect of others is soothing and beneficial.'

Negative leys are sometimes referred to as 'black streams'.

Dowsers who have investigated the phenomena report that illness, depression, unexplained accidents and even poltergeist-type activity can take place in their vicinity. It has been suggested that any major disturbance in the landscape, such as motorway-building, mining operations or quarrying, has the potential to create black leys. In such circumstances the normally beneficial influence of the ley can be changed into a malevolent power capable of wreaking havoc. Research indicates that not everyone who is exposed to a black ley is affected by its adverse influence. People who are psychic or sensitive can detect its malefic energy and could suffer physical symptoms ranging from severe headaches and emotional outbursts to even serious diseases such as cancer. Houses which are considered 'unlucky' or accident 'black spots' on roads could be explained by the existence of negative leys in the locality.

Once a black ley has been discovered, its potential for harm can be reduced or eliminated by a skilled dowser. He or she does this by using a technique known as 'earth acupuncture' which was known and practised by the *feng shui* practitioners of ancient China. The dowser first uses a pendulum or dowsing-rod to locate the route of the black ley. Angle irons or stakes bound with copper wire are then hammered into the ground at fixed points along the path of the suspect ley. This procedure reverses the polarity of the ley and renders it positive rather than negative.

Human nature being what it is, there is every possibility that in the distant past there were people who used the energy of the black leys for negative purposes. Since the beginning of the Christian era we have seen that certain groups following the esoteric tradition knew of the ley system and the sacred power centres. Some of these groups acted as guardians of the ancient wisdom, preserving its secrets for more tolerant times when the old knowledge would once again be renewed. Others who were aware of Earth Magic may have operated from less enlightened and selfless motives and used ley energy for anti-social and anti-evolutionary purposes.

The healing of the land is an important aspect of modern Earth Mysteries, especially with the demands society now makes on the countryside. Since the First World War, when mechanization first became a factor in modern farming, the pressures on the rural landscape have increased dramatically. Since the last war the establishment of the European Economic Community, with its radical agricultural policies and the requirements of consumers for a varied and fresh supply of foodstuffs, has led to intensive farming methods which have transformed rural areas. Increased leisure caused by unemployment and shorter working hours also poses a threat to the natural environments, as people living in cities increasingly see the countryside as their sparetime playground.

In the past thirty years thousands of miles of hedgerows have been uprooted as farmers have sought to increase the size of their fields to produce higher crop yields. The desire by the motorist to travel more and faster has prompted the construction of vast motorway systems across the country. Both the destruction of the hedges and road-building can have adverse effects on the flow of Earth energy from site to site across the landscape. Tarmac has been recognized as a sterile material which has a serious effect on natural energy flows. Attempts by humankind to control Nature and impose its collective will on the environment are a form of ecological fascism which increasingly will have a serious effect on the wellbeing of both our species and the planet unless positive steps are made to reverse this destructive trend.

The extent of the damage caused by our modern society on the environment is reflected in the impact made by progress on the sacred sites. Despite legislation passed protecting our ancient heritage, many of the lesser-known sites have been wantonly destroyed. This process began with the arrival of the Christian missionaries in the early centuries after the birth of Christ, who converted the pagan temples and shrines into churches. In the Middle Ages sacred sites, such as Avebury, were further desecrated, with their ancient stones used as a source of building-material or for road-construction. Today modern farming has threatened sacred sites, with standing stones removed from fields to make way for ploughing and burial mounds bulldozed in land-improvement schemes.

An additional pressure on ancient monuments has been caused by an increased awareness of our past heritage through education and commercial exploitation. This has been seen in the demands of the leisure industry, which has promoted sacred centres as tourist attractions. In the early 1980s the government responded to this by setting up English Heritage, a commission designed to protect ancient monuments while also operating as a marketing agency to promote them commercially for tourism. Unfortunately this policy has created serious problems for the sites, due to the fact that they have a spiritual significance to many people which is totally divorced from their modern image as tourist amenities.

The dilemma faced by our ancient sites as we enter the 1990s is graphically, if sadly, illustrated by the evolving fate of Stonehenge. When we first visited this site in the early 1960s, it was completely open to the public. A little old lady sat in a wooden hut selling postcards at 6d each, and the visitor was free to roam around the stones. Today entry to the henge is strictly limited, its boundaries are surrounded by barbed wire fencing, and every summer it is the scene of violent confrontations between riot police and the alternative culture.

Stonehenge has always been a subject of controversy in contemporary times. In the nineteenth century visitors to the site could hire hammers and chisels to chip pieces off the stones to take home as souvenirs. In 1899 the private owner of the site offered it for sale at the considerable sum (by contemporary standards) of £250,000. On New Year's Eve two of the stones from the outer circle fell down, and this was presumably taken as an omen, for the offer was withdrawn.

In 1901 permission was received from the Society for the Protection of Ancient Buildings and the Wiltshire Archaeological Society, who kept a watchful eye on the monument, to divert the old straight track which passed through the henge so that a fence could be erected around the circle. Visitors were allowed to enter the new compound on payment of a shilling and, attracted by the publicity of the proposed sale, about 3,000 did so in the first year. In 1906 the Druid Order, founded in the eighteenth century, was granted permission by the owner to hold their summer solstice ceremony at the circle at dawn when the sun rose over the stones.

Following the First World War, Stonehenge was finally sold, and its new owner presented the ancient monument to the nation in 1918 with the specification that the public should always have access to the site at any time. The supervision of Stonehenge was taken over by the Ministry of Public Works and eventually, with governmental re-organization, passed to the new Department of the Environment and then to English Heritage. In 1927 an area around the henge was purchased for £32,000 by the Stonehenge Protection Committee, who presented it as a gift to the National Trust. A further 650 acres were purchased in 1929 to prevent the commercialization of the area by private interests.

By the 1970s it was obvious that Stonehenge was fast becoming a victim of its own popularity. It was estimated that 2,500 visitors were entering the circle every hour, and the stones were being damaged by tourists climbing on them, carving them with graffiti and trampling the surrounding area. It was generally agreed that drastic action was needed to preserve the monument for future generations. In 1976 the matter was raised in the House of Commons, and a working party was set up, made up of representatives of the Department of the Environment, the National Trust, Wiltshire County Council and Salisbury District Council, to find a solution. Although various proposals were mooted, including restricting visiting-times, diverting traffic on the A303 road which passes the side and moving the car-park or putting it underground, very little was actually done to improve facilities at the henge. However, in March 1978 it was decided to fence off the circle and reroute visitors along a tarmac path which circled the stones.

In 1976 an extra factor in the Stonehenge controversy was added by the establishment of a free rock festival on land owned by the National Trust near the circle. This unofficial event attracted supporters of the counter-culture from all over the country, who gathered at Stonehenge not only to listen to rock music but to celebrate the midsummer sunrise as their megalithic ancestors had thousands of years ago. One of the festival organizers expressed his view in *The Times* in 1978 that Stonehenge was one of the most powerful spiritual centres in Europe. In reply to critics of the event he said, 'Holy land is holy land and our right to be on it cannot be denied.'

Initially the free festival appeared to be tolerated, and at first it seemed as if it would become a permanent fixture of the summer tourist season at Stonehenge. However, a series of sensational media reports claiming that widescale drug-dealing was going on at the festival and reports of damage to other ancient monuments in the area by Hells Angels riding motorbikes, caused a change in public and official opinion. In 1984 the National Trust and English Heritage obtained a court order banning the free festival. This step was to lead to a violent backlash as the alternative culture demanded right of access to the stones as laid down in the terms of the transfer of Stonehenge to the nation in 1918.

Since the 1950s the annual Druid ceremony had been attracting large crowds of sightseers, sometimes with unfortunate results. In 1956, for instance, the traditional ritual of greeting the sunrise was interrupted when smoke bombs were thrown at the white-robed Druids and a lady member of the order had her gown singed. This disturbance was to be nothing compared with the violence of the 1980s, when our television screens flickered with images of steel-helmeted riot police with batons and shields chasing long-haired 'hippies' across the Wiltshire countryside. The stones had become a battleground for a culture clash between the establishment and those following an alternative lifestyle, with neither side wishing to compromise or admit defeat.

The situation had become confused because the festival

organizers had established a modern tradition of celebrating the solstice at the circle, which included the naming of babies at the Heel Stone. Groups of neo-pagans also appeared on the scene, demanding access to the site, and celebrations of the winter solstice and the vernal and autumn equinoxes were peacefully held there, with scant media coverage, with the permission and assistance of English Heritage. The Druids, while not supporting the free festival, were fighting for their own rights to continue their midsummer ceremony in the face of mounting pressure from outside forces over which they had no control.

In 1988 English Heritage attempted to solve the impasse by issuing tickets for the dawn solstice ceremony, so that a selected and comparatively small number of people could enter the henge. A cordon of riot police was thrown around the stones to prevent unauthorized entry. This action was regarded as provocative by some of the large crowd which had gathered, and several hundred of them attempted to storm the police lines in the hope of enforcing public right of entry to the circle. In the resulting battle, stones and bottles were hurled at the riot police, who responded by baton-charging the crowd. Some women with children, who were authorized ticket-holders and had arrived on buses supplied by English Heritage, were caught up in the police charge and were attacked and beaten with batons.

The situation at Stonehenge is destined to be a protracted affair, with no easy solutions in sight. In March 1989 English Heritage announced that it had decided, on police advice, to close Stonehenge for the twenty-four-hour period of the summer solstice. The Chief Constable of Wiltshire said anyone crossing the county border to attend an illegal free festival would be turned back. The Druids, unable to cele-brate their dawn ceremony for the first time in eighty-three years, condemned the decision by English Heritage as a gross violation of religious freedom and said they would be taking the matter to the Court of Human Rights in Strasbourg. English Heritage said they regretted having to make the decision and still hoped peaceful solstice celebrations could be held at Stonehenge in the future.

What has happened at Stonehenge over the past fifteen
years is sadly indicative of the problems besetting our ancient
sites. At the White Horse of Uffington, for instance, the
thousands of visitors to the hill figure each year and the use of
the surrounding hill for leisure pursuits have prompted the
National Trust to erect signs requesting people not to walk on
the horse because it is becoming eroded. It seems only a
matter of time before the hill figure has to be fenced off to
prevent major damage from erosion. The Cerne Abbas giant
could also face similar problems caused by increased public
access in the next decade. In 1979 the National Trust carried
out restoration work on the giant costing £23,000. This they
claimed would preserve the figure into the early years of the
twenty-first century, providing tourist interest in the site does
not increase any faster.

Avebury's stone circle has also been the subject of public
controversy in recent years, due to both environmental and
commercial pressures. In 1986 it was reported that the heavy
flow of traffic on the A361 through the village was causing the
road to sink. English Heritage applied to Wiltshire County
Council to have the road rerouted away from the village and
the stones. A spokesperson commented, 'Apart from the
damage [to the road] it is absurd that 250,000 visitors a year
have to jump for their lives while walking around the circle.'

In 1988 Avebury was back in the news when the Kennet
District Council refused planning-permission for the construction of a new 'interpretation centre' on nearby Overbury
Hill. This centre would have consisted of three forty-foot-high
conical modules designed to imitate the shape of Silbury Hill.
In the same year the village was divided by plans formulated
by the new owner of the historic manor house to
commercialize it as a neo-Elizabethan tourist attraction.
Building-work was halted in the spring of 1989 pending the
outcome of a public inquiry.

A terrifying vision of the shape of things to come was
revealed in plans proposed by architects in 1989 working for

English Heritage. They suggested that the remains of a medieval church in Herefordshire should be enclosed in a glass pyramid to preserve it. There are also plans for a glass fibre roof in the shape of a tent to cover the ruins of a newly excavated abbey in Oxfordshire. Such radical proposals pose the question of how long it is before Stonehenge is encased in a plastic dome to protect it.

The plight of Britain's sacred sites surrounded with barbed wire and with limited public access is of concern to everyone who is interested in our ancient history. The measures to protect monuments of this type from vandalism, erosion and commercialization are obviously controversial and, some will say, have to be accepted if these sites are to survive for the benefit of generations to come. It is essential that the sites be protected, but in an environmentally sensitive way which allows easy access by those who are genuinely interested in their historical and/or spiritual significance.

The fundamental difference between the average tourist and the Earth Mysteries researcher or modern neo-pagan who visits the sites described in this book is their attitude to the ancient monuments. The casual visitor will find the site interesting as a historical relic and then pass on to some other tourist attraction on their holiday shopping-list. Those who are aware of the spiritual significance of stone circles, burial mounds and hill figures have different reasons for visiting them. This fact is not always appreciated by the official guardians who look after the sites on behalf of the people.

Returning to the subject of the healing of the land, which embraces both ecological considerations and the protection of sacred sites, some radical students of the Earth Mysteries have proposed the re-establishment of the old pagan ways as a legitimate way to protect both the ancient sites and the environment. To the outsider, who has little knowledge of these matters, some of the concepts presented under the cover of Earth Mysteries may appear bizarre. This is only because our modern way of life and perception of the natural world are so divorced from the old belief in the Earth and land as sacred.

Our ancestors firmly believed that every stone, tree and stream had its own guardian spirit or *genus loci*, the 'spirit of the place'. In pagan times these Nature spirits were often worshipped as gods and with the coming of the new religion were debased in folk-tradition as the elves, faeries and goblins of fairy-tales. The Czech-born bio-medical engineer Itzlak Bentov has used the theory that matter is impregnated with consciousness to explain the existence of these Nature spirits. He has claimed that consciousness can develop in allegedly inanimate objects over a period of millions of years by close contact with living organisms.

Bentov uses as an example a rock in a hypothetical desert. Through interaction with the animal life which exists in the desert environment, the rock gradually increases its level of primitive consciousness. For instance, a small rodent hunted by a bird of prey may seek shelter under the rock to escape its fate. Its feelings of gratitude will be transferred to the embryonic consciousness of the stone. The latter's ego will be further boosted when a bird makes a nest under the rock and lays its eggs. According to Bentov, the rock 'learns' that if it extends protection to other creatures they will respond with emotional feelings. This reciprocal process eventually creates what Bentov calls 'the spirit of the rock', a *genus loci* of pagan belief.

A quantum leap in the rock's consciousness follows when it encounters a primitive human who is sensitive to Nature. He or she instinctively feels there is something different or special about the rock. It is emanating a psychic vibration different from those of the other rocks around it. This human response enables the rock to evolve its consciousness to a higher level and possibly draw attention to its existence by externalizing some form of psychic or paranormal event in its vicinity. This attracts other humanoids who, according to Bentov's theory, stimulate the rock's consciousness with the energy from their nervous system. Before long the spirit of the rock has been transformed into a tribal god whose energy form is capable of manifesting in an archetypal image which can be seen by psychically sensitive humans.

The scientific proposition made by Bentov that matter is solidified energy with a capacity for conscious awareness is a key factor in understanding the spiritual philosophy behind the study of Earth Mysteries and especially the nature of the dragon power or Earth energy which flows along the ley lines between the sacred centres and which can be detected permeating the standing stones in the landscape.

We have encountered earlier in this book the strange, unexplained events which can be experienced at megalithic sites and which seem to include various levels of psychic phenomena. Dr Don Robins, who was one of the founder members of the Dragon Project set up to investigate leys and Earth energies, believes that these happenings can be explained by the molecular structure and energy fields of stone.

Dr Robins says that stone, rock and crystal are not lifeless or inert mediums. In common with other matter, stone is solidified energy which has a structure that may hold the key to the psychic phenomena experienced at ancient sites and explain why our ancestors both revered these places for spiritual reasons and used their natural energies for magical purposes. The folk-legends of standing stones which move and walk around and the tales of dancers on the Sabbath or witches' covens transformed into stone circles illustrate the belief that stone is not inanimate but is in some way 'alive'. It is Dr Robins' belief that the interaction of the human mind with the electromagnetic fields around stones can create dramatic changes in human perception and trigger altered states of consciousness. This process may release from the individual subconscious or the collective unconscious of the human mind archetypal images relating to the mystical experience and evolutionary origins of our species.

Belief in elemental forces and Nature spirits certainly coloured the attitude of our ancestors to the natural world. Today the Gaian hypothesis, the belief that Nature might be intelligent, and speculation concerning the extent of consciousness in matter are producing a new 'pagan' world view which is enlightened rather than atavistic. In this view humanity is seen as an integral part of Nature and interdependent on the other life forms inhabiting this planet. The concept of co-operation and communication with Nature spirits is one avenue being actively explored by those who believe in the spiritual approach to ecology.

The idea that humankind and the universe were one and that cosmic harmony has to be restored was fully accepted and understood by the ancients. They encapsulated this belief in the arcane science of sacred geometry which we examined earlier. While the ancient Chinese knew of the need for humans to live in ecological balance with their environment and encouraged this practice through the geomantic art of *feng shui*, we in the West have lost this esoteric knowledge and are the poorer in spirit for the loss.

The concept of Earth acupuncture to divert or harmonize black leys has already been mentioned but there are other positive steps which can be taken to heal the land. Alfred Watkins believed that the old beacon hills and their sacred fires were essential to the practical use of the ley system. Modern dowser and Earth Mysteries researcher Tom Graves has suggested that this concept should be revived. He believes that the network of beacon hills across the British countryside should be restored, along with the ritual practice of lighting sacred fires to mark the turning-points of the year at the solstices, equinoxes and cross-quarter days. It is his opinion that the restoration of this ancient tradition would create a national grid of Earth energy which would revitilize the land and its people.

Earlier in this book we touched upon the controversial subject of contact between early humans and extra-terrestrials. This subject has attracted sensational speculation which has tended to obscure any serious debate on the historical possibility of such contact ever happening in the distant past. The fact that many prehistoric stone circles were deliberately aligned to specific star systems and that the ancients had an advanced knowledge of astronomy would appear, to the converted, to be reliable evidence for a degree of interstellar communication thousands of years ago.

Some Earth Mysteries researchers have noted that unidentified flying objects (UFOs) are often sighted near megalithic sites or along the routes of known ley lines. Two areas of the country which have experienced large sightings of UFOs in recent years have been the so-called 'Welsh Triangle' in Pembrokeshire and the Warminster area of Wiltshire. Both these regions are renowned for their profusion of ancient monuments. Warminster, for instance, is close to Stonehenge, and many of its UFO sightings have been over local ancient monuments such as Cley Hill, whose legend of the Golden Ram of the Templars we examined earlier.

The alleged connection between UFOs and leys has led to speculation that the extra-terrestrial craft are powered by some kind of cosmic energy. Their tendency to fly along leys has suggested to believers that the UFOs can utilize the dragon energy as a power source for propulsion. The hippy image of huge, brightly lit starships hovering over Stonehenge may be a visual cliché but it is one which provides fascinating food for thought.

An alternative theory is the belief that, rather than using dragon energy as a power source, the UFOs themselves may be a product of Earth Magic. Research in recent years has indicated that UFO phenomena are concentrated near geological faults, during earthquake activity or at places where the Earth's magnetic field is weak or distorted. This has led to the belief that many UFOs sighted by observers are, in fact, 'earth lights' or pulses of electrical or electromagnetic energy created by seismic disturbances in the planetary crust.

The appearance of the alien occupants seen emerging from alleged UFOs and the other forms of strange phenomena reported near their landing-sites have been explained by leading Earth Mysteries researcher Paul Devereux as the product of a 'geophysical epiphany'. He suggests that UFOs are non-sentient, geophysical objects composed of energy which in some way interact with human consciousness to produce archetypal images. This interesting development in the range of dragon power opens up many exciting possibilities, although it fails to invalidate totally the possibility of an extra-terrestrial origin for UFOs.

As I hope this chapter has shown, the field of Earth Mysteries is a wide and universal one, embracing such diverse subjects as ecology and environmental protection, planetary healing, quantum physics, ancient religion, folklore and mythology. These different areas of research and experience combine to produce a holistic vision of the cosmos, with humanity and the planet as one unit operating in universal harmony.

Visits to the ancient sites described in this book should be seen in terms of the medieval pilgrimages to religious places. If you visit the sites wearing the mask of a tourist, their natural Earth Magic will mean nothing to you. Suspend belief in the normal and the rational which we are falsely taught to believe are the tools used to study the natural world. Approach them instead in the manner in which the ancients viewed them, and a whole new experience of enchantment, mystery and magic will open up to you.

Those pilgrims in search of ancient wisdom who visit our sacred centres to contact the dragon energy which flows along the lines of power know the meaning of the words of the Irish poet and mystic W.B. Yeats, who said, 'The borders of the mind are ever shifting, and many minds can flow into one another, and create or reveal a single mind, a single energy.'

BIBLIOGRAPHY

All books have been published in the UK unless otherwise indicated.

1 Ley Lines and Dragon Power
Behrand, Michael, *A Forgotten Researcher: Ludovic McLennan Mann* (Institute of Geomantic Research, 1977)
Devereux, Paul, and Thomson, Ian, *The Ley Hunters Companion* (Thames & Hudson, 1979)
Gerlach, Kurt, *Leys of the German Empire* (IGR, 1976)
Hadingham, Evan, *Early Man & the Cosmos* (Heinemann, 1983)
Heinsch, J., *Principles of Prehistoric Geography* (Zodiac House, 1975)
Hippisley Cox, R., *The Green Roads of England* (Methuen & Co, 1914)
Michell, John, *The Earth Spirit* (Avon Books, 1975)
Morrison, Tony, *Pathways to the Gods* (Michael Russell, 1979)
Pennick, Nigel, *British Geomantic Pioneers 1570-1932* (IGR, 1982)
Streit, Jacon, *Sun & Cross* (Floris Books, 1984)
Watkins, Alfred, *The Old Straight Track* (Methuen & Co, 1925)
      The Ley Hunter's Manual (Turnstone Press, 1983)

2 Astro-Archaeology
Balfour, Michael, *Stonehenge & its Mysteries* (Hutchinson, 1979)
Burl, Aubrey, *Prehistoric Astronomy & Ritual* (Shire Publications, 1983)
Hadingham, Evans, *Circles & Standing Stones* (Heinemann, 1975)
Hitching, Francis, *Earth Magic* (Cassell & Co, 1976)

Michell, John, *A Little History of Astro-Archaeology* (Thames & Hudson, 1977)
> *Megalithomania* (Thames & Hudson, 1982)
Ponting, M. and G., *The Standing Stones of Callanish* (privately printed, 1977)
Thom, A., *Megalithic Sites in Britain* (Clarendon Press, 1967)
> *Megalithic Lunar Observatories* (Clarendon Press, 1971)

3 Spiritual Geometry
Bond Bligh, F., *The Gate of Remembrance* (Thorsons, 1978)
Charpentier, Louis, *The Mysteries of Chartres Cathedral* (RILKO, 1972)
Critchlow, Keith, and Challifour, Graham, *Earth Mysteries: A Study in Patterns* (Research into Lost Knowledge Organisation, 1972)
Gimpel, Jean, *The Cathedral Builders* (Century Hutchinson, 1988)
Howard Gordon, Frances, *Glastonbury-Maker of Myths* (Gothic Image, 1982)
Lancaster Brown, Peter, *Megaliths, Myths & Men* (Blandford Press, 1976)
Michell, John, *City of Revelation* (Garnstone Press, 1972)
> *The New View over Atlantis* (Thames & Hudson, 1983)
Owen, Trefor, *Welsh Folk Customs* (Welsh Folk Museum, 1959)
Pennick, Nigel, *Sacred Geometry* (Turnstone Press, 1980)
> *The Ancient Science of Geometry* (Thames & Hudson, 1979)

4 Hill Figures
Alford, Violet, *The Hobby Horse & Other Animal Masks* (Merlin's Press, 1978)
Bergamor, Kate, *Discovering Hill Figures* (Shire, 1968)
Castleden, Rodney, *The Wilmington Giant* (Turnstone Press, 1983)

Collier, Mike, *The Sussex Elephant* (IGR, 1982)

Edwards, Lewis, *The Welsh Temple of the Zodiac* (IGR, n.d.)

Holden, E.W., *The Long Man of Wilmington* (Sussex Archaeological Society, 1971)

Lethbridge, T.C., *Gogmagog: The Buried Gods* (Routledge & Kegan Paul, 1957)

Maples, Morris, *White Horses & Other Hill Figures* (Alan Sutton, 1981)

Matchett, Edward, and Trevalyn, Sir George, *Twelve Seats at the Round Table* (Neville Spearman Ltd, 1976)

Newman, Paul, *Gods & Graven Images* (Robert Hale, 1987)

Oldfield Howey, M., *The Horse in Magic & Myth* (Castle Books, USA, 1968)

Taylor, Ian, *The Giant of Penhill* (Northern Lights, 1987)

5 *Earth Zodiacs and Mazes*

Ashe, Geoffrey, *The Glastonbury Tor Maze* (At the Foot of the Tree, 1979)

Caine, Mary, *The Glastonbury Giants* (privately printed, n.d.)
    The Kingston Zodiac (privately printed, 1978)

Kraft, John, *The Goddess in the Labyrinth* (Abo Akademi, Finland, 1985)

Pennick, Nigel, and Lord, Robert, *Terrestrial Zodiacs in Britain* (IGR, 1976)

Pennick, Nigel, *Labyrinths: Their Geomancy & Symbolism* (Runestaff, 1984)

Purce, Jill, *The Mystic Spiral* (Thames & Hudson, 1974)

Saward, Jeff, *The Book of British Troy Towns* (Caerdoria Project, 1982)

6 *Holy Wells and Sacred Springs*

Bord, Janet and Colin, *Sacred Waters* (Granada, 1985)

Bridgewater, Howard, *The Margate Grotto* (Kent Archaeological Society, n.d.)

Green, Dr Miranda, *The Gods of the Celts* (Alan Sutton, 1986)

Hardcastle, F., *The Chalice Well* (Chalice Well Trust, 1965)

Logan, Patrick, *The Holy Wells of Ireland* (Colin Smythe, 1980)

Shaw, Conan and Nellie, *The Shell Temple* (privately printed, 1954)

Stewart, R.J., *The Waters of the Gap* (Bath City Council, 1981)

7 Mounds and Pyramids

Atkinson, Richard, *Silbury Hill* (BBC Publications, 1967)

Brennan, Martin, *The Stars & the Stones* (Thames & Hudson, 1983)

Dames, Michael, *The Silbury Treasure* (Thames & Hudson, 1976)
The Avebury Cycle (Thames & Hudson, 1977)

Johnson, Ken, *The Ancient Magic of the Pyramids* (Corgi, 1979)

Lemesurier, Peter, *The Great Pyramid Decoded* (Compton Russel Ltd, 1977)

Mendelssohn, Kurt, *The Riddle of the Pyramids* (Thames & Hudson, 1974)

Schull, Bill, and Pettit, Ed, *The Secret Power of the Pyramids* (Fawcett Publications, Inc, USA, 1975)

8 Earth Magic

Balfour, Michael, *Stonehenge and its Mysteries* (Hutchinson, 1979)

Bentov, Itzhak, *Stalking the Wild Pendulum* (Wildwood House, 1978)

Devereux, Paul, *Earthlights* (Turnstone Press, 1982)

Graves, Tom, *Needles of Stone* (Turnstone Press, 1978)

Lovelock, Dr James, *Gaia: A New Look at Life on Earth* (Oxford University Press, 1979)

Robins, Dr Don, *The Secret Language of Stones* (Rider, 1988)

Roszak, Theodore, *Where the Wasteland Ends* (Doubleday, USA, 1972)

The following specialized magazines cover various aspects of Earth Mysteries, folklore and the pagan Old Religion:

The Cauldron
Caemorgan Cottage
Caemorgan Road
Cardigan
Dyfed

The Ley Hunter
P.O. Box 5
Brecon
Powys

Meyn Mamvro
51 Carn Bosavern
St Just
Penzance
Cornwall

Northern Earth Mysteries
103 Derbyshire Lane
Norton Lee
Sheffield
Yorkshire

Index